IRISH
GAELIC
TATTOO
HANDBOOK

THE
IRISH GAELIC TATTOO HANDBOOK

Authentic words and phrases
in the Celtic language
of Ireland

by
Audrey Nickel

bradan
press

Halifax, Nova Scotia

Bradan Press
Halifax, Nova Scotia, Canada
www.bradanpress.com
info@bradanpress.com

Disclaimer: This book is designed to provide information only. The author and publisher shall have no liability or responsibility to any person or entity regarding any loss or damage incurred, or alleged to have incurred, directly or indirectly, by the information contained in this book. Additionally, while the author and publisher have made every effort to ensure the accuracy of the information within this book at time of publication, the author and publisher do not assume and hereby disclaim any liability to any party for any loss, damage, or disruption caused by errors or omissions, whether such errors or omissions result from accident, negligence, or any other cause.

Library and Archives Canada Cataloguing in Publication

Nickel, Audrey, author
The Irish Gaelic tattoo handbook : authentic words and
phrases in the Celtic language of Ireland / by Audrey Nickel.

Includes bibliographical references and index.
Issued in print and electronic formats.
Text in English; some words and phrases in Irish Gaelic.
ISBN 978-0-9950998-8-3 (softcover).--ISBN 978-0-9950998-9-0 (EPUB).--
ISBN 978-1-988747-00-2 (Kindle).--ISBN 978-1-988747-01-9 (PDF)

1. Irish language--Handbooks, manuals, etc. 2. Irish language--
Terms and phrases--Handbooks, manuals, etc. 3. Irish language--
Glossaries, vocabularies, etc.--Handbooks, manuals, etc. 4. Tattooing--
Handbooks, manuals, etc. 5. Words in art--Handbooks, manuals, etc.
I. Title.

PB1214.N53 2017 491.6'2 C2017-901974-0
C2017-901975-9

Front and back cover illustrations © 2017 by Pat Fish
Pat Fish is known internationally for her Celtic tattoo art, bringing the ancient illuminated manuscripts and patterns from standing stones alive in skin. View her work at luckyfish.com and luckyfishart.com.

Back cover author photo © 2017 by Paul Schraub, Santa Cruz, CA, paulschraubphoto.com

Figures © 2017 by Emily McEwan-Fujita

Irish-language editors:
Pól Ó Braoin, facebook.com/braoin.obraoin
Cathal Ó Míocháin

Printed by KDP

To my loving and long-suffering husband, Tony, who has cheerfully supported me in my Irish studies for more than 13 years.
Tá mo chroí istigh ionat, a stór!

Special thanks to my friend Bríd Éilis Ní Fhlatharta for her help and advice during the writing of this book.

Table of Contents

Introduction   1

    The reason for this book   2

    Where's the artwork?   2

Chapter 1: What is Irish Gaelic?   3

    Irish, Gaelic, or Irish Gaelic?   3

    A brief history of the Irish language   5

    The decline of Irish under English rule   6

    The status of the Irish language today   7

    Irish dialect differences   8

        The traditional dialects   9

        The Official Standard   9

        Urban Irish   9

    Interesting features of the Irish language   10

        The verb comes first   10

        Words can change… a lot   11

        New beginnings   11

        "No" doesn't mean no   12

    Conclusion   12

Chapter 2: Irish Writing and Symbols   13

    Traditional Irish writing   13

    Ogham   14

    Celtic knotwork   15

    Other popular symbols   16

Chapter 3: Tattoo Translation "Fails"   17

    Drug-free disaster   17

    The girl made sorrowful by a bad translation   18

    My soul what?   20

Daddy's little who?   22

Don't be a meme   24

Chapter 4: Translation Issues and Advice   25

Translation issues   25

    "Simple" isn't always so simple   26

    First step in translation: what do you mean?   26

    Which word works best?   27

    When it works but it doesn't   27

    Song lyrics and poetry   28

Translation advice   28

    Glossary translations: the three big "don'ts"   28

    Adapting translations or finding new ones   29

    Cultural cautions   31

    Bottom line: your tattoo, your responsibility   32

Chapter 5: The Irish Tattoo Glossary   33

How to use the glossary   33

The Irish tattoo glossary   38

    Place, identity and heritage   38

    Family   40

    Love and friendship   50

    In memoriam   55

    Religious and spiritual   57

    Courage, honour, and service   66

    Work, activities, and identities   69

    Emotions, qualities, and concepts   71

    Personal mottos and sayings   74

    Quotes from movies, TV, and literature   78

    Traditional Irish sayings and proverbs   80

Resources   83

Glossary Index   87

Introduction

When I first began learning Irish in 2004, I was amazed and a bit baffled at the number of people who wanted to incorporate Irish words or phrases into tattoo designs. And, like other Irish learners and speakers before and since, I had one question: why in Irish?

The reasons people gave were as diverse as the requestors, but the majority of them fell into six categories:

- To express pride in their own Irish heritage
- To honour a loved one's Irish heritage
- To satisfy a personal aesthetic
- To express solidarity with Irish political situations
- To make their tattoo unique
- To express a religious or spiritual path

Many of these reasons are reflected in the wide range of glossary choices in the final chapter, while the other reasons are explored in Chapters 2, 3, and 4.

The reason for this book

If you purchased this book, you or someone you care about may be planning an Irish-language tattoo. The aim of the book is to provide you with the information you need to ensure that you get a tattoo you can be proud of. The final chapter of this book is a glossary of Irish words, phrases, sayings, quotes, and translations of common requests. You may well find the translation you're looking for there.

This book is much more than a dictionary, though. It's also a guide to the Irish language and, to an extent, to the people who speak it.

I sincerely hope that this book will give you a better understanding of the Irish language and why we who speak it want so ardently to preserve it. Perhaps you'll even decide to join us and begin learning Irish yourself.

Where's the artwork?

You'll notice that this handbook does not contain any tattoo artwork, other than a few basic examples of Irish symbols. The choice of artwork for a tattoo is extremely personal, and I urge you to work closely with your tattoo artist to come up with a design that suits you. An internet search for "Irish," "Gaelic," or "Celtic" designs will yield plenty of ideas.

Be aware, however, that not all so-called Irish symbols have the meaning that artists assign to them, and that not all symbols represented as "Celtic" are actually Irish. In Chapter 2, I describe some of the designs and symbols that people may incorporate into Irish-language tattoos and talk a bit about what they mean.

I also invite you to explore the work of tattoo artist Pat Fish, who designed the cover art for this book. Pat's website, luckyfishart.com, features a wide range of Celtic tattoo artwork, and readers of this book may use the coupon code IRISH1 to receive a discount on the purchase of her tattoo designs.

Chapter 1

What is Irish Gaelic?

Irish, Gaelic, or Irish Gaelic?

Outside of its home country, Irish is a language with a bit of an identity problem. If you happen to mention in the U.S. that you're learning Irish, for example, you're likely to get one of the following reactions:

- "Do you mean you're learning to speak with an Irish accent?"

- "You speak Irish? Me too! Top o' the mornin' to ye, faith and begorrah!"

- "They have their own language?"

- "Don't you mean 'Gaelic'?"

- "Isn't that a dead language?"

A surprising number of people outside of Ireland don't seem to know that the Irish have ever spoken any language other than English. Those who do know don't seem to know what to call it or even that it's still spoken.

In Ireland, of course, this isn't a problem. The official name of the language in English is "Irish", and that's what they call it. Some even get irritated by the term "Irish Gaelic."

The matter of what to call the language is a problem when you're talking to people outside of Ireland, though. Once I offered a class called "Irish for Travelers" in California and ended up teaching a group of people who had no idea they would be learning a different language! They were planning a tour of Ireland and thought they would be learning about Irish customs.

To add to the confusion, some people in Ireland, particularly older people, do call the language "Gaelic." They're not wrong. In Irish it's called *Gaeilge*. In its linguistic classification, Irish is one of the Gaelic (or Goidelic) languages (see the next section). The problem is that when the word "Gaelic" is used by itself in English, by convention it refers to modern Scottish Gaelic, which is the Celtic language of Scotland.

While Irish and Scottish Gaelic are very closely related, they are different languages. The comparison I like to use is Spanish and Portuguese. For the most part these two languages are not mutually intelligible, particularly in speaking. The similarities between them are clear to anyone who reads or hears the two languages together, however, and there is some mutual intelligibility between people who speak Scottish Gaelic and speakers of the Ulster dialect of Irish (more information on dialects is found later in this chapter).

Those of us who are speaking to an audience outside of Ireland are left with a problem: what do we say to make it clear that we're talking about a non-English language specific to Ireland without causing confusion?

The compromise is to use the term "Irish Gaelic," even though that's not a term you would hear in Ireland. This makes it clear that we are speaking about a language, that this language is native to Ireland, and that it's neither Scottish Gaelic nor English.

Among ourselves, however, we simply call the language "Irish," which is how I'll be referring to it in the rest of this book.

A brief history of the Irish language

Irish is one language in the Celtic family of Indo-European languages. Other members of the Celtic family include Scottish Gaelic, Manx, Welsh, Cornish, and Breton.

These languages originated among a loosely affiliated group that the Greeks called Keltoi and that we know as the Celts (pronounced with a hard C: "Kelts").

Sometimes people are under the misapprehension that "Celtic" is synonymous with "Irish." This is untrue. The Celtic label encompasses much more than just Irish. The Celts were never a single, united people, but rather a collection of groups with similar material culture styles and languages that shared certain features.

The Celtic language family has two branches: the Q-Celtic or Goidelic (Gaelic) branch and the P-Celtic or Brythonic (British) branch. "British" in this sense is not synonymous with "English," but refers specifically to the Celtic peoples and languages that came to inhabit the region of Brittany and parts of the island of Great Britain.

The languages of the P-Celtic group are Welsh (*Cymraeg*), which is spoken in Wales; Cornish (*Kernowek*) which was spoken in Cornwall, and is undergoing revitalization efforts; and Breton (*Brezhoneg*), which is spoken in the region of Brittany in what is now France.

The languages of the Q-Celtic group are Irish (*Gaeilge*), which is spoken in Ireland and, to some extent, in the Canadian provinces of Newfoundland and Ontario; Scottish Gaelic (*Gàidhlig*), which is spoken in parts of Scotland and in the Canadian province of Nova Scotia; and Manx (*Gaelg*) which is spoken in a revitalized form on the Isle of Man.

Irish, Scottish Gaelic, and Manx are considered "sister" languages because they all evolved from a common ancestor: Middle Irish. By the 12th century, Middle Irish had begun to evolve into three separate varieties that were to become Modern Irish, Scottish Gaelic, and Manx. Because of this relatively recent shared linguistic ancestor, the three languages of the Q-Celtic group resemble one another more closely than do the languages of the P-Celtic group.

Irish was a purely oral language for much of its early history. With the exception of short inscriptions in Ogham (see Chapter 2), writing was brought to Ireland with Christianity and the monasteries. This allowed for the preservation of a large body of traditional lore and laws that might otherwise have been lost as Irish gradually succumbed to the effects of colonization.

The decline of Irish under English rule

Well into the 19th century, Irish was still the native language of most of the people of Ireland. Colonization had already taken its toll, however, as the native Irish people were pushed to the far west of the island through war, forced relocation, the usurpation of land by English landlords, and the plantation of colonists loyal to England.

Perhaps the two greatest blows to the language in Ireland, however, were the imposition of an English national school system and the so-called "Irish Potato Famine" (known in Irish as *An Gorta Mór*, The Great Hunger).

The English national school system was established in Ireland in the late 18th century when the oppressive "Penal Laws" were lifted. Among other things, these laws forbade education "in or out of Ireland" to any Catholic, which included most native Irish speakers. Teachers were encouraged to literally beat the Irish out of children. Many Irish parents cooperated with this Anglicization of their children, recognizing that an education and the ability to speak the language of the occupiers was the only way their children could hope to have a better life than their parents.

The Great Hunger of 1845–1852 was the result of seven years of failure of the potato crop upon which the Irish depended as a staple. Despite being commonly called the "The Irish Potato Famine," the Great Hunger wasn't technically a famine at all. Plenty of food was being produced in Ireland at the time and being shipped out of the country under English law. The Great Hunger ended in the death, transportation (exile), or emigration of approximately two million people, most of them Irish speakers. Those who made it to the U.S., Canada, England, or Australia, or even to the big cities in Ireland, saw little point in maintaining and passing on the language, as English was what they and their children needed to survive.

More recent blows to the Irish language have come from dissatisfaction with the way the language has traditionally been taught in schools, by emphasis on other languages, and by the government's often half-hearted approach to preserving the language.

The status of the Irish language today

Today Irish is the primary home, work, or community language for approximately 1% of the population of the Republic of Ireland. The regions in which Irish is spoken as a daily language are known collectively as the Gaeltacht, and are located mostly along the western edge of the island.

Irish isn't limited to the Gaeltacht, however. Legally, it is the first official language of the Republic of Ireland (English is the second). Irish is required on certain types of public signs, such as road signs. It is a required subject in school, and approximately 94,000 people claim to use Irish daily outside of the school system.

Irish speakers enjoy a dedicated TV station (TG4) and several radio stations that broadcast mostly or entirely in Irish. There has also been a resurgence of Irish in the urban areas, including the formation of several Irish-medium schools known as *Gaelscoileanna*. A small but increasing group of people, though not native speakers themselves, are choosing to raise their children through Irish.

The status of Irish in the Republic, however, should not be overstated. Many Irish people are ambivalent or even downright hostile toward the language, which they view as a waste of time and resources. And much of the Irish on signage, both public and private, is embarrassingly bad.

In Northern Ireland, the six counties of Ireland that have remained a part of the United Kingdom, Irish is a recognized minority language. It first received official recognition there in 1998 under the Good Friday Agreement, which ended the three-decade period of violent conflict known as "The Troubles."

Irish shares minority-language status in Northern Ireland to a somewhat lesser degree with Ulster Scots, a variety of the Germanic language known as Scots that is spoken in parts of Scotland. Ulster Scots was brought to Ireland by Scots, mostly Presbyterians, who began migrating to the area around 1600. This migration accelerated during the "Plantation of Ulster," which began officially in 1609. Protestants from both Scotland and England were encouraged to settle in the northern part of the island of Ireland in an attempt to quell dissent from the native chieftains. You will often see both Irish and Ulster Scots on signage throughout the province.

An increasing number of people in Northern Ireland across the political and religious spectrum are involved with learning and promoting the Irish language.

Irish dialect differences

A dialect is a form of a language that is spoken in a particular area and uses some of its own particular words, grammar, and pronunciations. Dialects are not considered different languages, but the criteria for determining whether something is a dialect or a language are fluid, and often more political than linguistic.

The Irish dialects don't differ greatly from one another. A comparison I like to use is the English spoken in New York City compared to the English spoken in Atlanta, Newfoundland, London, or Sydney.

These dialects all have their own words and expressions. Sometimes they use the same words differently. Sometimes they pronounce certain words differently. But at the end of the day they're all English, and they are all mutually intelligible with a bit of practice.

The same is true with Irish dialects. Most learners begin by learning a mixture of dialects, and only specialize in one when they're reasonably advanced, if they wish. A dialect is most significant to people who are interested in a particular region.

For the most part, dialect differences don't play a big role in tattoo translations. The kinds of words and phrases that people seem to like for tattoos don't tend to vary much among dialects. In the glossary (see Chapter 5), any significant dialect variations will be noted.

Some people do have a strong affinity for one part of Ireland or another, however, so here is some basic information on Irish dialects.

The traditional dialects

There are three primary traditional Irish dialects: Ulster, which is spoken in the northern part of the island; Connacht, which is spoken in the west; and Munster, which is spoken in the south. There are also regional dialects within the primary dialects.

The province of Leinster, in the eastern part of the island, used to have its own dialect, but that dialect is now extinct. Most Irish speakers in this area are either transplants from other regions or second-language learners who may speak any dialect, or sometimes a mixture of dialects.

The Official Standard

You can't be around Irish speakers or learners long without hearing a comment or complaint about *An Caighdeán Oifigiúil*, the official standardized form of the language.

An Caighdeán was developed in an effort to reconcile the dialects into a standard form for the purposes of education, official documents, etc. The problem is that this standard form has never been universally adopted, and is disliked and even disdained by many Irish speakers.

The reality is that no one actually speaks *An Caighdeán*. The standard is only a written form, not a spoken form, so it doesn't even address the matter of different pronunciations in the regional dialects. Some Irish learning programs will refer to themselves as standardized, but even these have to make dialect choices when it comes to pronunciation, word choice, and common phrases.

Urban Irish

So-called "Urban Irish" is a relatively new phenomenon. Broadly speaking, it refers to the Irish spoken by second-language learners, mostly in the cities.

At its best, Urban Irish is a vibrant and exciting phenomenon. Most people I know who would identify as Urban Irish speakers are passionate about the language. They are constantly working to improve their Irish. Often they have made the choice to live their lives as much as possible through the medium of Irish. They're raising their children through Irish. They are typically the ones who are driving the *Gaelscoil* (Irish-medium education) movement, as well as promoting the language through conversation groups and classes. In many ways, they are the future of the language.

The flipside, however, is that some people who identify as Urban Irish speakers directly translate a lot of English idioms into Irish (*Béarlachas*). They tend to use English pronunciations in their Irish speech, and may claim not to understand some native Irish speakers.

It's hard to say what direction the language will ultimately take. There's no doubt that, if Irish is to survive, it needs to be embraced by people throughout Ireland, and can't be simply a Gaeltacht museum piece. It has to grow and evolve. At the same time, heavily Anglicized pronunciation and lack of sensitivity to native Irish idiom isn't a direction in which most Irish speakers would like to see the language moving.

Interesting features of the Irish language

People often ask me "How does Irish differ from English?" Sometimes I'm tempted to say "You mean other than being a completely different language, with a different vocabulary, grammar, syntax, and mode of expression? Not much, I guess!"

However, I know that they're just curious about how Irish may differ from other European languages with which they may be more familiar. Here are some of its more interesting features, many of which it shares with other Celtic languages:

The verb comes first

Irish is what is known as a VSO (verb-subject-object) language. Put simply, in a basic Irish sentence the verb comes first. In contrast, English is an SVO (subject-verb-object) language, that is, the subject comes first. For example, in English we might say: "The dog ate the food." "The dog" is the subject, "ate" is the verb, and "the food" is the object of the verb.

In Irish, however, we'd say: "*D'ith an madra an bia.*" "*D'ith*" is the verb "ate," "*an madra*" is the subject, "the dog," and "*an bia*" is the object, "the food." So the sentence translates literally as "Ate the dog the food."

Words can change... a lot

Compared to English, Irish is much more inflected. This means that the forms of Irish words may change significantly, both in spelling and pronunciation, based on their function in a sentence or phrase.

In English we're accustomed to fairly simple inflections, such as adding an "s" to a word to make it plural or an apostrophe plus an "s" to make it possessive. In Irish, however, the changes can be much more profound. For example, "*teach*" (pronounced "chakh") means "house." "*Seán*" (pronounced "shawn") is a man's name. If you want to say "Seán's house," though, you say "*Teach Sheáin*" (pronounced "chakh HYA-in").

Such changes are extremely common in Irish, which is one reason you can't just swap out one word for another in a translation.

New beginnings

In English we expect only the ends of words to change. In Irish, as you saw in the example above, the beginnings of words frequently change as well, depending on how the word is used. These changes are called "initial mutations."

There are two types of these changes in Irish. One is *séimhiú* (also known as lenition or softening) which is represented in modern writing by placing an "h" after the consonant. You saw an example of this in "*teach Sheáin*" above. Lenition is indicated by placing a dot over the consonant in the older style of writing known as *Seanchló* or *Cló Gaelach* (see Chapter 2). You'll often see this in older texts, or on decorative signs such as those on pubs.

The other initial mutation is *urú* (also known as eclipsis), in which a lowercase letter or combination of letters is written in front of the first consonant of a word. The sound of the lowercase letter eclipses, or replaces, the sound of the consonant. For example, "*i*" (pronounced "ih") means "in" and "*Dún na nGall*" (pronounced "DOON-nung-all") means "Donegal" (a county and city in Ireland). If you want to say "in Donegal," though, you say "*i nDún na nGall*" (pronounced "ih NOON-nung-all").

It's really important, when you're copying out a translation for a tattoo (or for any other use), that you remember that these letters must be lowercase. I can't count the number of times I've seen something like "I Ndún na Ngall" because someone's computer spellchecker imposed English capitalization rules on Irish.

"No" doesn't mean no

One interesting feature of Irish that takes a lot of people by surprise is that it doesn't have dedicated words for "yes" and "no." In fact, the way to say "yes" or "no" changes, depending on the question.

When Irish speakers want to say "yes" or "no" in answer to a question, they simply restate the verb used in the question, in a positive form for "yes" or in a negative form for "no." For example, if I were to ask someone "*An dtuigeann tú mé?*" ("Do you understand me?"), the answer would be "*Tuigim*" ("I understand") or "*Ní thuigim*" ("I don't understand").

If I were to ask "*Ar mhaith leat cupán tae?*" ("Would you like a cup of tea?") however, the answer would be either "*Ba mhaith*" ("Would like") or "*Níor mhaith*" ("Wouldn't like").

Because of this, simple English phrases such as "No means no" or "Just say no" are longer and fairly complicated in Irish.

Conclusion

These are just a few of the many grammatical differences between Irish and English. Irish is a beautiful, complex, ancient, and living language. Learning all you can about it is one way to show your pride and interest in Irish culture, and will enhance your enjoyment of your tattoo.

Chapter 2

Irish Writing and Symbols

This chapter covers the most basic aspects of the Irish writing system: the alphabet and fonts. It also reviews the most widely-used Irish symbols and their meanings. These aspects of the language and culture are vital to understand when planning an Irish tattoo.

Traditional Irish writing

Contrary to what some people think, Irish is not written using symbols or runes, and it never has been. Since the 5th century CE, Irish has been written using the Latin script (the same alphabet that we now use to write English) minus a few letters. Traditionally, Irish hasn't used the letters j, k, q, v, w, x, y, or z, and has only used the letter h in certain grammatical contexts. Some modern loan words, however, are written using these letters in contemporary Irish.

Until the late 1950s, Irish was written in a very stylized form of the Latin alphabet called *Cló Gaelach* or *Seanchló*. Most of the letters are easily recognizable, but there are some, such as "s" and "r," that can look quite different in some fonts. It can take a bit of practice to read it easily.

You'll still see this type of writing in older books and manuscripts, as well as on signs throughout Ireland, especially on pubs. It can make for a lovely, authentic look in a tattoo. Here's an example, *Éire Go Brách* ("Ireland Forever") using Bunchló, one of the many Irish-style fonts available:

Éire Go Brách

Traditionally, instead of an "h" after a consonant, a dot would be written over the consonant. Here's what that looks like in Bunchló:

Éire Go Bráċ

There are several sites on the internet where you can download *Seanchló* fonts, some classic and some very modern, which you can then use in a word processing or art program to design your tattoo. One of the best of these sites is gaelchlo.com. The site is written in Irish, but I explain how to use it in the Resources section at the back of this book.

Be careful, though. Some modern so-called "Celtic" fonts, such as American Uncial, are problematic because the dot over the lowercase "i" is rendered as a slash, making it look like an acute accent ("í"). Since Irish words are misspelled if accents are placed where they don't belong, fonts such as these are not a good choice for writing in Irish. Make sure the font you choose uses a dot instead of a slash, or has no dot over the lowercase "ı" (this would be the more traditional form of writing it in Irish).

Ogham

Often when people ask about Irish "runes," what they're actually thinking of is not Germanic runes but Ogham (pronounced "oh-m," similar to the meditation mantra).

Ogham is a very old alphabet that was used mainly for inscriptions in Primitive Irish and Old Irish, as well as Latin, Pictish, and Old Welsh. It is a phonetic alphabet that consists of short lines and slashes along a longer line. It was used mainly in the 5th through 7th centuries CE for carving names on stones that may have marked graves, memorial sites, or territories. Later it was used in manuscripts.

Figure 1: An example of Primitive Irish written in Ogham. It reads "LIE LUGNAEDON MACCI MENUEH," which translates to "The stone of Lugnaedon son of Limenueh" (adapted with permission from omniglot.com)

There are websites that will convert Latin letters to Ogham. However, they will not *translate* English words to Irish. They only *transliterate* or re-write those English words in the Ogham alphabet. Ogham letters are not necessarily pronounced the same as English letters, though, so the best you can hope for is an approximation of your English phrase.

Most contemporary Irish speakers are not going to be able to help you much with Ogham. If you ask about it on an Irish language forum, someone may be able to guide you (see Resources).

Celtic knotwork

There is probably no motif more popular for Irish tattoos than Celtic knotwork, and for good reason: it's beautiful, readily identifiable as Irish, and can be incorporated into just about any kind of design. These designs were created through fusion with classical Mediterranean and Anglo-Saxon art motifs, and were used by the early Christian monks to decorate such iconic manuscripts as The Book of Kells. They were re-popularized during the Celtic Revival of the 19th century, and remain popular with Irish and Celtic enthusiasts.

One thing to be aware of is that there's no such thing as a "Celtic motherhood knot," or "the Celtic knot for brothers," or a Celtic knot representing any abstract concept. Although jewelry makers and T-shirt designers may claim otherwise, the various knot designs have no known Celtic cultural meanings. If you like a particular knot design, by all means use it! But use it because you like it, not because you've been told that it stands for something.

In contemporary tattoo art, knots are often incorporated into such symbols as hearts, shamrocks, etc. An elaborate design like this can give your tattoo a beautiful touch but, once again, they are modern designs and have no inherent traditional meaning.

Other popular symbols

Ireland's ancient culture features many recognizable symbols, any of which could be incorporated into a tattoo design. Some you are probably familiar with include the harp, the high cross (a type of ringed cross), the claddagh (two hands holding a crowned heart), and the shamrock (shamrocks always have three leaves; don't confuse them with four-leafed clovers). Other images from Irish legends include The Salmon of Knowledge (*An Bradán Feasa*) and the Irish wolfhound, which is often used to symbolize bravery. The cover art for this book combines symbols by blending a fanciful winged wolfhound with the harp. Such combinations can be useful for personalizing a design.

Another very old symbol that can make for a nice tattoo is the spiral, particularly the triple spiral or triskelion. Examples of this can be found on ancient monuments throughout Europe, including the Stone Age monument at Newgrange in Ireland. We don't know exactly what spirals meant in the pre-Celtic culture of Ireland, but this symbol and the motif of "three" continued to be used in Celtic art across Ireland and north and west Britain.

With so many options available, it should be possible for you and your artist to come up with a tattoo design that you will find meaningful and enjoyable, and that you will be proud to show to others.

Figure 2: Example of a triskelion or triple-spiral image similar to the ones found at Newgrange

Chapter 3

Tattoo Translation "Fails"

One reason I wrote this book is that I want you to get an accurate translation, both for your sake and for the sake of the language. The other reason is to help prevent disasters such as the real-life translation "fails" below. Getting a tattoo in a language you don't speak is always risky, and the examples that follow illustrate exactly how wrong a translation can go if you don't know what you're doing.

Drug-free disaster

The tattoo in Figure 3, which is meant to say "drug-free," has become notorious on the internet as an example of translation gone wrong. The person claims to have gotten the translation from friends in Ireland.

The first thing that any Irish speaker would notice is the apostrophe in the first word. Apostrophes are used in Irish the same way they are in English: in a contraction to indicate an omitted letter. However, there is no contraction in this phrase. Instead this apostrophe was used incorrectly to represent an accent mark over the "A." The correct spelling of the word is "*drugáil.*"

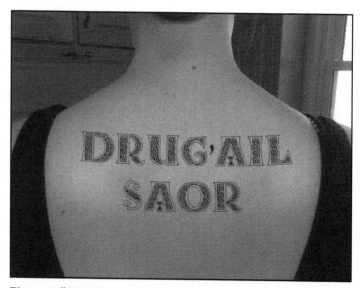

Figure 3: "*DRUG'AIL SAOR*", an incorrect Irish tattoo design

Another problem is that "*drugáil*" isn't the noun "drug." It's a verb form that, depending on context, can mean "to drug" or "drugging." The correct word for the noun "drug" in Irish is "*druga*," the plural of which is "*drugaí*."

The word "*saor*" does mean "free," but you wouldn't say "drug-free" in Irish by putting *saor* after the noun. In fact, often when *saor* comes after a noun, it means "cheap." That's right. What this person has written on her neck is "cheap drugging," although with the mis-spelling it looks more like "CHEAP DRUGG'ING."

If you wanted to say "drug-free" in Irish you might say "*saor ó dhrugaí*," "free from drugs" (see glossary entry 372 in Chapter 5). Unfortunately, there is no way to fix this tattoo other than cover-up or laser removal.

The girl made sorrowful by a bad translation

"The girl made lovely by sorrow" is a common translation request, and that is apparently what the tattoo in Figure 4 was supposed to mean. Unfortunately this person got it very wrong.

Read by itself this translates roughly to "The girl prays to whom beauty..." or "The girl prays who has beauty...". It's clearly a sentence fragment, taken out of context, and the exact meaning would depend on the rest of the sentence.

It turns out that this is a paraphrase of part of a line in an Irish poem, "*An tAmhránaí*" (The Singer), written by Louis de Paor. The original line of the poem translates to "The girl with the beauty of sorrow in her face prays that he will be without a spouse until he finds her." Here's what it looks like in Irish: "*Guíonn an cailín a bhfuil áilleacht an bhróin ina gnúis go mbeidh sé gan chéile go bhfaighidh sé í.*"

What may have happened here is that the person who did the so-called translation just took the first six words of the line in Irish, assuming that they corresponded to the six words of the English paraphrase "the girl made lovely by sorrow."

Unfortunately, you can never assume that a sentence in another language will have the same word order as a sentence in English. Chapter 1 explains that the verb comes first in an Irish sentence. "*Guíonn*" (prays) is the first word here. A literal, word-for-word translation of this line would be: "Prays the girl who has beauty the of-sorrow in her face that will be he without spouse until will find he her."

Figure 4: "*Guíonn an cailín...*", an incorrect Irish tattoo design

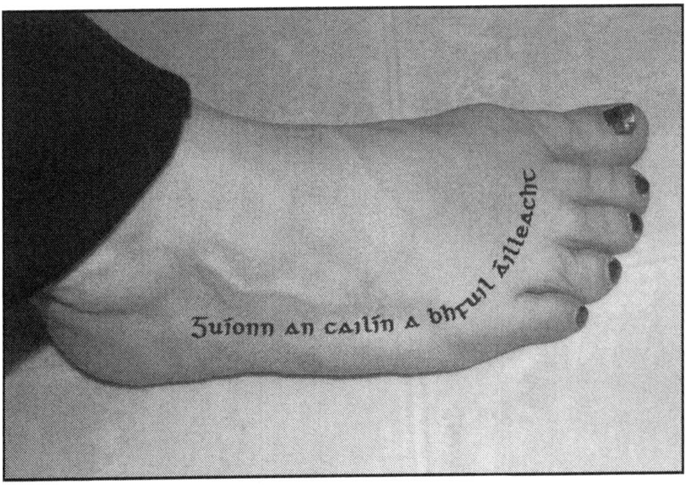

There are several possibilities for fixing this tattoo. The easiest one would be to add the words "*an bhróin ina gnúis*" to the end. This would amount to "the girl with the beauty of sorrow in her face prays," implying that she prays regularly or constantly. If she's a spiritual person, this might work for her.

Another option, if she's looking for love, would be to complete the original line of poetry by adding the words "*an bhróin ina gnúis go mbeidh sé gan chéile go bhfaighidh sé í*" which would then read "the girl with the beauty of sorrow in her face prays that he will be without a spouse until he finds her" (see glossary entry 402 in Chapter 5).

My soul what?

There's so much wrong with the tattoo in Figure 5, it's hard to know where to start. Let's get the simplest problem out of the way first: the symbols. Those aren't shamrocks, they're four-leafed clovers. The shamrock, one of the best-known symbols of Ireland, only has three leaves. This comes from a legend that St. Patrick used the shamrock to illustrate the concept of the Christian Holy Trinity, the three-in-one, to the high king at Tara.

Four-leafed clovers are considered lucky all over the world because of their rarity, but they don't have any special affiliation with Ireland. The popularity in the U.S.A. of the Gold Rush-era phrase "the luck of the Irish" may be the reason for the present-day confusion between the three-leafed Irish shamrock and the four-leafed lucky clover.

Now on to the linguistic problem. "Soulmate" and "soulmates" are popular Irish tattoo requests. These words are commonly sought for other romantic uses as well, including wedding rings and wedding invitations. They also give Irish translators a major headache.

To begin with, "soulmate" isn't an Irish concept—it comes from Greek philosophy, specifically from Plato's *Symposium*. Plato envisioned original human beings as having four legs, four arms, a single head with two faces, and two sets of genitalia. In *Symposium*, Zeus, fearing that humans would threaten the gods, cut them in half. Now, so the story goes, each half longs for its other half: its "soulmate."

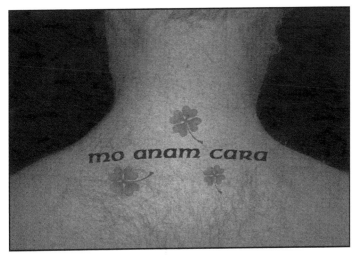

Figure 5: "*Mo Anam Cara*," an incorrect Irish tattoo design

A similar concept and term never evolved in Irish. Even in other European countries, the meaning of "soulmate" is typically different from in North America: Europeans are more likely to see soulmates as very close friends, whereas Americans are more likely to view soulmates as lovers fated to be together.

In an effort to capitalize on the popular conception of love as finding one's soulmate, jewelers, possibly with some help from misguided "Celtic" Christianity enthusiasts, have contrived a term that cannot exist grammatically in Irish: "Mo Anam Cara." It's such bad Irish, it's close to nonsense.

You'll see this bogus phrase all over the internet and on jewelry and cards in Irish shops all over the world, even in Ireland. It always makes Irish speakers cringe because not only does it not mean "My Soulmate" (or, as it's more commonly rendered, "My Soulfriend"), it's also a grammatical nightmare.

It's possible that this odd construction stems at least in part from a misreading of the title of Irish poet and philosopher John O'Donohue's popular 1997 book *Anam Ċara: Spiritual Wisdom from the Celtic World*. Note the dot over the letter "C" in *Ċara*. In contemporary Irish writing, this would be written *Anam **Chara*** with an h instead of the dot. Most writings about the book, as well as major editions of the book itself, omit the dot over the C but don't add the "h," which is incorrect in Irish.

Additionally, "*anamchara*" is typically written as a compound word in Irish, not two separate words. It's possible that the two-word form is a mistake or poetic license on the part of the author. *Anamchara* presents a problem of its own, however, in that its definition in Irish is not "soul friend" or "soulmate" but rather "confessor or spiritual advisor."

During the early days of Christianity in Ireland, one monk would have another monk whom he trusted to guide his spiritual formation and to hear his confessions. That person was his *anamchara*. In modern usage, *anamchara* has come to mean "confessor," that is, the priest who hears your confession before mass.

If all the above weren't enough to make Irish speakers cringe, even the word for "my" is written incorrectly. "*Mo*" (my) becomes *M'* before a vowel, so "my soul" is "*m'anam*," not "*mo anam*."

So what can you do if you still want "soulmate" in Irish for a tattoo? There are options, depending on what aspect of soulmate-hood you want to emphasize. For a close friend, you might want to say "*buanchara*"—"eternal/everlasting friend." For "soulmate" in a romantic sense, some options include "*buanghrá*" and "*síorghrá*," "eternal or everlasting love."

Lastly, for either sense of "my soulmate," you could also use the grammatically correct "*cara m'anama*"—"friend of my soul." You'll find more options for "soulmate" in glossary entries 164 through 168 in Chapter 5.

Daddy's little who?

At least the tattoo in Figure 6 got the shamrock right. There is a major design flaw, however: the font makes the dots on the lowercase "i"s look like acute accent marks (fadas). I talked about this a bit in Chapter 2. Irish has both accented and unaccented vowels, so the difference between an accented "í" and an unaccented "í" is significant. "*Daid*" and "*cailin*" look misspelled here. There should be only one accented "í" in those words, and that's the second "í" in "*cailín.*"

Once again, however, the bigger problem is with the phrase "Daid Beag Cailín" which is nonsensical. The person wearing this tattoo was going for "Dad's Little Girl." Unfortunately, as with the "soul-mate" tattoo discussed earlier, the tattoo designer just picked words out of an Irish dictionary and stuck them together in English word order with no possessive. It makes as much sense as "Dad Girl Little" in English.

In Irish, when one word modifies another, the modifier typically follows the word that it modifies. This is the case for most adjectives, such as "*beag*" ("small/little"). So one correct way to write this would be "*Cailín Beag Dhaid*" or if "Daddy" is preferred, "*Cailín Beag Dhaidí*" (Daddy's Little Girl).

Figure 6: "*Daíd Beag Caílín,*" an incorrect Irish tattoo design

Sometimes tattoo seekers ask for "Daddy's Girl" without the "Little". This is one of those times when a literal translation just doesn't work well. The most commonly used word for "girl"—"*cailín*"—can also mean "girlfriend." A fluent friend of mine once said that, even though he would know what was meant, if he saw "*Cailín Dhaidí*" his first thought would be "Daddy's bit on the side." (Ew!)

Including "little" makes it less ambiguous, so if you're aiming for something along the lines of "Daddy's Girl," I suggest you go with "Daddy's Little Girl," or one of the other options in glossary entry 52 in Chapter 5.

Unfortunately, there's no way to correct this particular tattoo, other than removing or covering up the words and starting over.

Don't be a meme

There are many more examples of real-life tattoo translation fails in Irish, and in other languages as well. Your tattoo is meaningful and important to you. You want it to be correct—not something that goes viral on social media for people to laugh at. In Chapter 5 you'll find the tools you need to make sure you design a tattoo that you can show off proudly.

Chapter 4

Translation Issues and Advice

Now we're ready to get down to the nitty-gritty: the things you absolutely must keep in mind when designing your tattoo. This chapter explains some of the challenges of translating from one language to another, and tells you what you should and should not do when seeking a translation.

Translation issues

Most people who seek tattoo translations don't understand how challenging translation between languages can be. You might have a few words—maybe a short paragraph, or a few lines from a song. You look at it and it seems fairly straightforward. Every language has its own way of expressing things, however, so what seems simple to express in one language may be quite complicated in another.

As languages go, Irish is fairly wordy compared to English. Often we have to rephrase things in Irish in a way that uses a greater number of words than the English original. For example:

English: I love you

Irish: *Tá grá agam duit*
(literally translates as "Is love at-me for-you")

Idiom is another consideration. An idiom is an expression particular to a given language or region. It's surprising to me sometimes that people expect uniquely English and sometimes uniquely American idioms to work in another language. You can translate them word for word, and many Irish speakers will get what you were trying to say because they also speak English, but they won't really make sense in the context of the Irish language and culture.

For example, take the word "sweetheart." You wouldn't translate that literally into Irish. It would sound ridiculous: "*croí milis*" (literally "a sweet heart"). Instead you'd use a native Irish endearment, such as "*cuisle mo chroí*" ("pulse of my heart").

"Simple" isn't always so simple

A while ago a woman I'll call "Jane" approached me through social media seeking confirmation for a couple of Irish translations she had found on the internet. She was seeking a translation for the phrase "forever family," and, as is typically the case with translations that are the result of an internet search, the translations she had found were wrong. I helped Jane through the process of getting an accurate translation, and I asked her if I could use her request to illustrate the difficulties of translating a seemingly simple English expression into Irish.

First step in translation: what do you mean?

The translation process almost always begins with questions, and I had a few for Jane: "What does 'forever family' mean to you? Are we talking about this as it is used in adoption circles, to mean a family group that has adopted you or that you have adopted, and with whom you will have a permanent relationship?" Jane said no; she was referring to the family into which she was born.

I asked, "In that case, could this possibly be reworded as 'family forever'?" Jane said yes. Her goal was to express pride in and hope for her family, now and in the future.

These two different concepts would be expressed very differently in Irish, so knowing which one Jane intended was essential. Even the simplest phrase can have multiple meanings in different contexts or to different people. Jane was very cooperative, and worked closely with me to determine exactly what "forever family" meant to her. We did end up rewording it as "family forever."

Which word works best?

The next thing I had to ask Jane was "What do you mean by 'family'?" This may seem to be an odd question, but it's an important one.

In English, "family" is a broadly inclusive word whose meaning we derive from context. Irish, on the other hand, has several words that can mean "family," depending on who (or what) you want to include in that definition. Jane and I discussed the various options and came to the conclusion that "*muintir*," a word meaning "people" or "folk," was the best choice for what she meant by "family." *Muintir* can be used to describe the entire extended family, or as a friend of mine once put it, "The entire family-reunion crowd, throwing in neighbors, ancestors, and possible descendants for good measure."

I suggested to Jane that saying "my family" (*mo mhuintir*) might make her meaning clearer to Irish speakers, and she agreed to that change.

Finally I asked her which phrase she preferred for "forever": "*go deo*" or "*go brách*." These phrases are synonyms, and neither has any particular regional affiliation, so it was just a matter of which she preferred aesthetically. She settled on "*mo mhuintir go brách*"—literally "my family/people forever."

When it works but it doesn't

The other major issue with translation is that you can have something that is grammatically correct, and that corresponds more or less literally to what you want to say, but that isn't something a native Irish speaker would ever say.

However popular it is among tattoo seekers, "family forever" is an American concept, suited to American English. Usually, if Irish speakers want to express the same basic sentiment, they will either mention a particular family or a place connected with a family, most likely followed with "*abú*"—"onward"—rather than "forever." These preferences represent Gaelic cultural concepts of family.

When it comes to this kind of culture clash, you have to give some serious thought to how important a literal or semi-literal translation is to you versus something that is authentically Irish.

Song lyrics and poetry

Poetry, including song lyrics, presents a unique set of translation problems. To get a good poetry translation you need a translator who is not only fluent in both languages, but is also a poet in his or her own right. For this reason, amateur translators are often reluctant to attempt these translations.

One of the problems is that, even if a relatively literal translation is possible, it's not going to be particularly poetic, nor will it rhyme or scan like the original.

The other issue is that poetry is often ambiguous, and any given line can carry multiple levels of meaning that may not be clear to someone who isn't familiar with the poet or songwriter, or with the cultural milieu in which the poem or song was written.

If you're seeking a poetry translation, be prepared for a lot of questions and a lot of work. The more context you can supply, the better. And, if you really want it to sound both poetic and natural in Irish, be prepared to settle for a paraphrased version.

Translation advice

If you're like most people, you're eager to jump right into the glossary and start designing your tattoo. Please read this first. It can save you a lot of heartache and embarrassment.

Glossary translations: the three big "don'ts"

When using a translation from the glossary in this book, the three most important pieces of advice are:

Don't change the punctuation, capitalization, or spelling. I cannot emphasize this enough. Irish spelling rules are very different from English and may seem strange to you. Some words may seem to have more letters than you think they should have. Sometimes the same word will be spelled slightly differently in one sentence than in another, based on its role in the sentence. Additionally, Irish grammar rules sometimes require different capitalization or punctuation than that to which you may be accustomed. Moreover, beware of the auto-correct feature on your computer or phone, which can make sneaky and unwelcome mistakes such as changing "i" to "I."

Don't swap out words or change the word order. Again, Irish often expresses things differently from English. If you try to change the word order or substitute a word, you stand a very good chance of getting it wrong.

Don't change the accent marks. The accent mark in Irish is called a "*síneadh fada*" ("long accent"), or *fada* for short, and it serves an important purpose: it tells you how the word is supposed to be pronounced. The *fada* always slants to the right, by the way; if you come across Gaelic writing with a left-slanting accent, it's Scottish Gaelic. I once encountered someone who put an accent on every single letter in her prospective tattoo design because she thought they were pretty, but accent marks aren't there for decoration. Leaving the *fada* out if it should be there, or putting one in where it doesn't belong, is considered a misspelling, and can even change the meaning of a word.

What this all adds up to is, if you want to change something from the glossary, even if you think it would be a minor change, get help. I'll tell you how to do that next.

Adapting translations or finding new ones

It's possible that what you want to say isn't in the glossary. Or perhaps you've found something you like in the glossary, but you want to change it up a bit. In either case, you're going to need help. Here is some important advice about that:

Don't try to do it yourself. Irish does not work at all like English (see Chapter 1). If you don't speak the language, don't even think of trying to do your own tattoo translation with a dictionary.

Don't use an automatic translator. Machine translation doesn't handle Irish or other minority languages at all well. It may be fine for getting the gist of something you're reading in a foreign language, but if you're looking for a translation for something permanent or important, it's best avoided.

Don't rely on an internet search. There's a lot of really bad Irish on the internet, including all the examples in Chapter 3. If you don't speak the language you have no way to tell the good from the bad.

Also, because of the ways in which words change in Irish depending on how they are used, even if a word you may find is correct in the sentence where you found it, it may not be correct once you incorporate it into your tattoo phrase or sentence.

Don't trust something you've found in a novel, poem, or song. Let me repeat: there's a lot of really bad Irish out there, and a lot of authors simply don't bother to get the Irish they use in their books checked by actual Irish speakers. Sometimes what they claim is Irish isn't Irish at all! The same is often true of poets and songwriters.

Don't use a translation from a friend or family member, at least not without having the translation checked by other Irish speakers, before having it inked. It's a shame, but some people misrepresent (or perhaps over-estimate) their level of Irish. Just because someone took Irish in school doesn't mean that he or she is fluent. You also risk being the butt of a bad joke if someone deliberately gives you a bogus translation as a prank, and you get it tattooed without having it verified. It does happen.

Here are a few steps you can take to get a good translation, or a reliable verification of something you've found here or elsewhere:

Do consider seeking out a professional translator. This would be the ideal first step. Not only would you get a good translation, you would be supporting the Irish language in a very tangible way. Also, if you are willing to spend a lot of money on a tattoo, why not spend a bit more to guarantee that it is spelled and worded correctly? See the "Resources" section for information on finding professional translators.

If hiring a professional translator is out of the question, here are some "Do's" you can use to make the internet work to your advantage:

Do seek out an Irish discussion forum. An online discussion forum is a much better for this kind of in-depth translation help than are social media platforms such as Facebook or Twitter. The slower pace and threaded format of an old-school forum makes it easier for both tattoo seekers and prospective translators to keep track of suggestions and corrections.

Do be certain that any forum you find is willing to do tattoo translations. Many are not. As of this writing the only one I'm aware of that is explicitly willing to take on tattoo translations is the Irish Language Forum (see Resources). Others may arise as time goes by. If you're not certain that a particular forum is open to doing this kind of work, ask before you post your request, either by contacting a moderator or administrator or by asking in an introductory post.

Do make it clear from the outset that you're seeking a translation for a tattoo. Forum members will be extra careful if they know you're getting something permanent done and aren't just asking out of curiosity.

Do be sure to tell them what other translations you may have found and where you got them. They can tell you right away if what you have is correct, what alternatives there may be, and if your source is a reliable one. If it's wrong, they can explain why.

Do observe "The Rule of Threes." Do not use a translation until three forum regulars have agreed on it.

Do be patient. Don't wait until the day, or even the week, before your tattoo appointment to start looking for a translation! The five scariest words for anyone who does tattoo translations are "My appointment is this afternoon." Rushing can lead to mistakes.

Do be especially careful if, despite the advice above, you decide to give social media a try. If you do decide to try to get a translation from a social-media site, it's important that you be extra vigilant. Try to work out who the more experienced and reliable speakers are—it might be worth your while to send a private message to a moderator or administrator asking for this information. Stay on top of your request, read all comments, and, as with a discussion forum, observe the "Rule of Threes." Most importantly, don't go with a particular translation just because it got a lot of "likes" or up-votes. There may be trolls at work, and in any case translation is not a popularity contest.

Cultural cautions

Don't expect every Irish person to be thrilled with your tattoo. Ireland is no longer the place your grandfather left. Both the Republic of Ireland and Northern Ireland are modern, forward-looking countries, and people often have little patience with the heavily romanticized version of Ireland that many Irish-Americans cherish, and that tourism marketing campaigns enthusiastically promote.

Some may even consider your use of the Irish language to be a form of cultural appropriation, especially if you're not interested in learning the language, or if you've used it just to be "cool" or "different."

Do keep in mind that Irish culture is not the same as Irish-American culture. The Irish-American community sometimes embraces stereotypes that people in Ireland may find offensive, particularly those regarding drunkenness, fighting, or quaintness.

Do be especially careful when it comes to politics. People of Irish descent all over the world may have their own opinions about Irish political and territorial unity, but it's for the people who live there, many of whom have lived under the spectre of war for generations, to decide what needs to be achieved and how best to achieve it. Since the Good Friday Agreement of 1998 the people of Northern Ireland have been working toward peaceful resolutions of their differences and, increasingly, both sides are embracing the Irish language as a part of their shared heritage. If you do get a tattoo relating to Irish political and territorial unity, be aware that others, even those you may think are on "your side," may find it offensive. At the very least, they may consider their politics to be none of your business. Personally, I don't do translations that relate to Irish politics, and you will find none in this book.

Bottom line: your tattoo, your responsibility

In the final analysis, this is your tattoo, and the ultimate responsibility is yours. The glossary entries have been checked by professional Irish copyeditors, but it is up to you to follow the guidelines and suggestions of this book as you plan your tattoo.

Chapter 5

The Irish Tattoo Glossary

The entries in this glossary have been compiled from many different sources, including internet discussion forums, songs, dictionaries, and lists of traditional Irish proverbs.

How to use the glossary

The glossary contains over 400 individual words and phrases organized into categories. Within categories the entries are organized more or less alphabetically, but with thematic variations taking precedence.

Not every glossary entry will be relevant or appealing to every reader. Tattoos are intensely personal, and what one person finds beautiful, another may find offensive. Simply disregard the entries that don't reflect your own beliefs, taste, or values. The inclusion of an entry in the glossary does not imply that the author or the publisher agrees with the concept or sentiment it expresses.

How to search

You can search the glossary in several ways. The first is to browse through the relevant categories. For example, if you're looking for a Bible verse or the Wiccan Rede, you would browse the "Religious and Spiritual" section.

Another way is to browse the glossary index. Each glossary entry has a unique number. In the index, every English word or phrase is listed alphabetically, followed by the unique number of the glossary entry or entries that contain that word or concept.

Format of entries

Each entry follows the same format. First, the English word or phrase is given in bold type. In some entries, the part of speech to which the word belongs (for example, "noun" or "adjective") or other important information may also be listed on this line.

The Irish translation follows in regular type. Some entries may have more than one possible translation. In these cases, if there is a difference in meaning, or if a translation is specific to a certain area, it will be noted. Sometimes the literal meaning of each will be given so you can select which works best for you. Otherwise you may use whichever you find more aesthetically pleasing.

In some cases an entry may be followed by a double asterisk (**). These entries are grammatically correct, but are expressed in a way that would not be usual among native Irish speakers. You'll need to decide whether you want something that corresponds directly to your request or if you would be happier with something that is more natural in Irish.

Some entries will include a note that gives important background information about the original phrase or the translation. Pay attention to these notes before you make your final decision on a tattoo. For example, under the entry for "Family," you'll find a note referring the reader to Chapter 4, where the Irish-language concept of family is discussed.

Spelling

There may be spelling differences within the variations of a given translation. These are not mistakes; they are required by Irish grammar. For example:

Father, Son, Holy Spirit
Athair, Mac, Spiorad Naomh

The Father, the Son, and the Holy Spirit
An tAthair, an Mac, agus an Spiorad Naomh

In the name of the Father, and of the Son, and of the Holy Spirit
In ainm an Athar, agus an Mhic, agus an Spioraid Naoimh

These variations are required by the role each word plays in each phrase. For more on why this happens, see Chapter 1. There may also be spelling variations between dialects.

Parts of speech

Where necessary to avoid confusion, some single-word glossary entries are designated as a noun, an adjective, or a verb. These categories, known as "parts of speech," describe words by their function in a sentence.

Pay special attention to the parts of speech if you plan to combine different words into a single tattoo design that takes the form of a series of words, such as "family, love, life" or "friendship, love, loyalty." Make sure that all the words are the same part of speech, for example, all nouns. Do not mix nouns, verbs, and adjectives.

Important distinctions

Pronouns, short words such as "me," "you," and "he" that can take the place of nouns, can be different in Irish. For example, Irish has two different words that correspond to the second-person pronoun "you," depending on whether you envision yourself speaking to or about one person or multiple people. Unlike some other European languages, the Irish singular does not imply "informal" and the plural does not imply "formal."

Imperative verbs, verbs that are used to issue commands, appeals, or instructions, also differ according to number. Imperative constructions will be designated "*sing.*" (second-person singular) or "*pl.*" (second-person plural). You may select either the singular or plural version, depending on whether you envision the command or appeal in your tattoo as being addressed only to yourself or to a group of people.

The word for "my" when used in reference to people or things differs in Irish depending on whether you envision yourself speaking about the person or thing or directly to the person or thing. The first option is written using the possessive adjective "*mo*" (my), much as we would write it in English. The second is written using the word "*a*," which corresponds to the word "O" often found in English poetry and prayers. This second option is known as the vocative case, and is required in Irish when addressing someone or something directly. For entries that can use both options, the two choices will be listed separately, and the vocative form will be labeled "*voc*."

Capitalization

When you see a lowercase consonant or cluster of consonants in front of another consonant at the beginning of a word, that letter or cluster *must* always be written lowercase, no matter how you write the rest of the word. For example, "*Déanta i gCeanada*" may be written "*DÉANTA I gCEANADA*," but never, ever "*DÉANTA I GCEANADA.*"

The same is true of some consonants that appear before vowels. For example "*a hathair*" (her father) would be written "*a hAthair*" if the word "*athair*" (father) were to be written with an initial capital.

This is an extremely important feature of the Irish language, so if you want to change the capitalization of any entry in the glossary, please seek the help of a professional translator or Irish language internet forum. Do not attempt to do it on your own.

Bible verses and religious expressions

All Bible verses are taken from *An Bíobla Naofa*, an authorized Irish translation of the Bible. Christian prayers and rituals (such as the Sign of the Cross) are taken from a standardized form of the Mass in Irish, with suggested variations from a native Irish speaker. Pagan expressions have been suggested by practitioners of contemporary Paganism and translated with the help of the people of the Irish Language Forum (see Resources).

Longer entries

Some entries, such as poems or prayers, may consist of several lines. In those cases I've broken these entries into separate lines, which you can use by themselves if you don't want to use the entire entry. For example, in the Our Father, aka The Lord's Prayer:

Our Father who art in Heaven
Ár nAthair atá ar Neamh

Hallowed be thy name
Go naofar d'ainm

You can use the entire prayer or use these lines individually, as you prefer.

Irish proverbs

This section lists some traditional Irish proverbs, known in Irish as "*seanfhocail*"—literally "old words." There are many more Irish proverbs in existence. I've chosen those that are frequently requested, and those that seem to be most suitable for tattooing. If you want to explore this category further, I recommend the "Proverbs" section on the Daltaí na Gaeilge website (see Resources).

adj.	adjective (a word describing a noun)
lit.	literally, word-for-word
noun	noun (a word for a thing, person, or place)
sing.	second person singular ("you" to one person)
pl.	second person plural ("you" to multiple people)
voc.	directly addressing someone ("O my darling")
**	grammatically correct, but not normal for native Irish speakers to say
Connacht, Munster, or Ulster	the Irish dialect area of that particular translation (in contrast, *standard* indicates the translation belongs to no particular dialect area)

Figure 7: Abbreviations and labels used in the glossary

The Irish tattoo glossary

Place, identity and heritage

1. **Heritage**
   Oidhreacht

2. **Homesickness** *or* **Nostalgia** *or* **Parting sorrow** *or* **Longing**
   Cumha

3. **If you're lucky enough to be Irish, you're lucky enough.****
   Má tá sé d'ádh ort a bheith i do Ghael, tá do dhóthain den ádh ort *(lit. If it's your luck to be Irish, you have your fill of luck)*
   Má tá sé d'ádh ort a bheith i d'Éireannach, tá do dhóthain den ádh ort *(lit. If it's your luck to be born or reside in Ireland, you have your fill of luck; Éireannach instead of Gael implies birth or residence in Ireland rather than ethnic Irishness*

4. **Ireland**
   Éire

5. **Ireland, land of my heart**
   Éire, tír mo chroí

6. **Ireland, love of my heart**
   Éire, grá mo chroí

7. **Ireland forever**
   Éire go brách *(standard)*
   Éirinn go brách *(Munster and Connacht dialects)*

8. **I am Irish**
   Is Gael mé
   Is Éireannach mé *(Éireannach instead of Gael implies birth or residence in Ireland rather than ethnic Irishness)*

9. **Irish** *(noun, see entry 8 on Gael vs. Éireannach)*
   Gael
   Éireannach

10. **Irish** *(adj., see entry 8 on Gael vs. Éireannach)*
    Gaelach
    Éireannach

11. **Irish-American** *(noun, a person born in the U.S.A. of Irish descent)*
    Gael-Mheiriceánach**

12. **Irish boy** or **Irish lad** *(see entry 8 on Gael vs. Éireannach)*
    Buachaill Gaelach
    Buachaill Éireannach

13. **Irish-Canadian** *(noun; a person born in Canada of Irish descent)*
    Gael-Cheanadach**

14. **Irish girl** or **Irish lass** *(see entry 8 on Gael vs. Éireannach)*
    Cailín Gaelach
    Cailín Éireannach

15. **Land of my birth**
    Mo thír dhúchais *(lit. Land of my birthright/heritage)*

16. **Land of my heart**
    Tír mo chroí

17. **Land of my soul**
    Tír m'anama

18. **Luck of the Irish**** *(see entry 8 and Chapter 3)*
    Ádh na nGael
    Ádh na nÉireannach

19. **Made in America of Irish parts**
    Déanta i Meiriceá as páirteanna Éireannacha

20. **Made in Canada of Irish parts**
Déanta i gCeanada as páirteanna Éireannacha

21. **Made in Ireland**
Déanta in Éirinn (*lit. Made in Ireland*)
De dhéantús na hÉireann (*lit. Of Irish manufacture*)

22. **Made in the United States of Irish parts**
Déanta sna Stáit Aontaithe as páirteanna Éireannach
Déanta sna S.A.M. as páirteanna Éireannach (*lit. Made in the U.S.A. of Irish parts*)

23. **My heart is in Ireland**
Tá mo chroí in Éirinn

24. **Proud to be Irish** (*see entry 8 on Gael vs. Éireannach*)
Bródúil as a bheith i mo Ghael**
Bródúil as a bheith i m'Éireannach**
Gael bródúil (*lit. Proud Irish person*)
Éireannach bródúil (*lit. Proud Irish person*)
Gael mórtasach (*lit. Proud Irish person*)
Éireannach mórtasach (*lit. Proud Irish person*)

25. **Tradition**
Traidisiún
Seanchas (*specifically ancient tradition or lore*)

Family

26. **Baby** (*only in the sense of infant*)
Leanbán (*may also be spelled* Leanbhán)
Leanbh (*also used for young children in general, and as a term of endearment*)
Babaí (*a borrowing from English, but widely used; particularly common in Ulster*)

27. **My baby** *(if speaking about your baby; see entry 26 on the meanings of different words for baby)*
Mo leanbán *(may also be spelled* Mo leanbhán*)*
Mo leanbh
Mo bhabaí

28. **My baby** *(voc., see entry 26)*
A leanbhán
A leanbh
A bhabaí

29. **Our baby** *(if speaking about your baby)*
Ár leanbán
Ár leanbh
Ár mbabaí
(If you want this to sound as if you're talking to your baby instead, see entry 28)

30. **Brother**
Deartháir

31. **Brothers**
Deartháireacha

32. **My brother**
Mo dheartháir

33. **My brother** *(voc.)*
A dheartháir

34. **Dear brother** *or* **Beloved brother**
Deartháir dil

35. **Brothers forever**
Deartháireacha go brách
Deartháireacha go deo

36. **The oldest brother**
An deartháir is sine

37. **The middle brother**
An deartháir i lár báire

38. **The youngest brother**
An deartháir is óige

39. **My brother, my friend**
Mo dheartháir, mo chara

40. **My brother, my friend** *(voc.)*
A dheartháir, a chara

41. **My brother, my best friend**
Mo dheartháir, cara mo chléibh *(lit. My brother, my bosom friend)*
Mo dheartháir, mo dhlúthchara *(lit. My brother, my close friend)*

42. **My brother, my best friend** *(voc.)*
A dheartháir, a chara mo chléibh
A dheartháir, a dhlúthchara

43. **I am my brother's keeper**
Is coimeádaí mo dhearthár mé

44. **Children**
Páistí
Leanaí
Clann

45. **My children**
Mo pháistí
Mo leanaí
Mo chlann

46. **Our children**
Ár bpáistí
Ár leanaí
Ár gclann

47. **My children are my world** *or* **My children are my life**
Is í mo chlann mo chuid den tsaol *(lit. My children are my share of life)*

48. **Cousin** *(first cousin)*
Col ceathrar

49. **My cousin**
Mo chol ceathrar

50. **Dad**
Daid *(standard)*
Deaide *(Connacht or Ulster)*

51. **Daddy** *or* **Papa**
Daidí

52. **Daddy's little girl**
Cailín beag Dhaidí**
Peata beag Dhaidí *(lit. Daddy's little pet/darling)*
Iníon bheag Dhaidí *(lit. Daddy's little daughter)*
Iníon bheag a Daidí *(lit. Her Daddy's little daughter)*
Iníon a hathar *(lit. Her father's daughter)*
Iníon m'athar *(lit. My father's daughter)*

53. **Daughter**
Iníon

54. **Daughters**
Iníonacha

55. **My daughter**
M'iníon

56. **My daughter** *(voc.)*
A iníon

57. **My daughters** *or* **My girls**
Mo chlann iníonacha

58. **Our daughter**
Ár n-iníon

59. **Our daughters**
Ár gclann iníonacha

60. **My daughters are my world** *or* **My daughters are my life**
Is í mo chlann iníonacha mo chuid den tsaol

61. **My beautiful daughter**
M'iníon álainn

62. **Two beautiful daughters**
Beirt iníonacha áille

63. **Three beautiful daughters**
Triúr iníonacha áille

64. **Four beautiful daughters**
Ceathrar iníonacha áille

65. **Family** *(see Chapter 4)*
Teaghlach *(household, immediate or nuclear family)*
Muintir *(extended family, including ancestors and descendants, lit. "people/folk")*
Clann *(the children of a family, members of a race, or descendants of a common ancestor)*

66. **Family above all** *(see entry 65 and Chapter 4)*
An teaghlach chun tosaigh ar gach uile ní
An mhuintir chun tosaigh ar gach uile ní

67. **Family first**** *(see entry 65 and Chapter 4)*
Tús áite don teaghlach *(lit. family first)*
Tús áite don mhuintir *(lit. family first)*
An teaghlach an chéad rud *(lit. family is the first/ primary thing)*
An mhuintir an chéad rud *(lit. family is the first/ primary thing)*

68. **Family forever**** *(see entry 65 and Chapter 4)*
An teaghlach go brách
An teaghlach go deo
An mhuintir go brách
An mhuintir go deo

69. **My family forever**** *(see entry 65 and Chapter 4)*
Mo theaghlach go brách
Mo theaghlach go deo
Mo mhuintir go brách
Mo mhuintir go deo

70. **Family, faith, forgiveness** *(see entry 65 regarding two words for family; faith here means religious belief)*
An teaghlach, an creideamh, an maithiúnas
An mhuintir, an creideamh, an maithiúnas

71. **Father**
Athair

72. **My father**
M'athair

73. **My father** *(voc.)*
A athair

74. **Dear** *or* **beloved father**
Athair dil

75. **Fatherhood**
Athaireacht

76. **My father's son**
Mac m'athar

77. **His father's son**
Mac a athar

78. **Grandchild**
Garpháiste

79. **Grandchildren**
Garpháistí

80. **Granddaughter**
Gariníon

81. **Granddaughters**
Gariníonacha

82. **Grandfather**
Seanathair

83. **My grandfather**
Mo sheanathair

84. **My grandfather** *(voc.)*
A sheanathair

85. **Grandpa** *or* **Granddad**
Daideo

86. **Grandmother**
Seanmháthair

87. **My grandmother**
Mo sheanmháthair

88. **My grandmother** *(voc.)*
A sheanmháthair

89. **Dear grandmother** *or* **Beloved grandmother**
Seanmháthair dhil

90. **Granny** *or* **Grandma**
Mamó

91. **Grandson**
Garmhac

92. **Grandsons**
Garmhic

93. **Honour thy father and thy mother** *(Bible, Exodus 20:12, first half of verse)*
Tabhair do d'athair agus do do mháthair onóir *(direct quote from* An Bíobla Naofa: *Give to thy father and to thy mother honour)*
Tabhair onóir do d'athair agus do do mháthair *(paraphrase: Give honour to thy father and to thy mother)*

94. **Honour thy father**
Tabhair onóir do d'athair

95. **Honour thy mother**
Tabhair onóir do do mháthair

96. **Mom**
Mam
Mama

97. **Mommy** *or* **Mammy** *or* **Momma**
Mamaí

98. **Mother**
Máthair

99. **My mother**
Mo mháthair

100. **My mother** *(voc.)*
A mháthair

101. **Dear mother** *or* **Beloved mother**
Máthair dhil

102. **Motherhood**
Máithreacht

103. **Her mother's daughter**
Iníon a máthar

104. **My mother's daughter**
Iníon mo mháthar

105. **His mother's son**
Mac a mháthar

106. **My mother's son**
Mac mo mháthar

107. **My mother and father**
Mo mháthair is m'athair

108. **My parents**
Mo thuismitheoirí

109. **Sister**
Deirfiúr

110. **Sisters**
Deirfiúracha

111. **My sister**
Mo dheirfiúr

112. **My sister** *(voc.)*
A dheirfiúr

113. **Dear sister** *or* **Beloved sister**
Deirfiúr dhil

114. **Sisters forever**
Deirfiúracha go brách
Deirfiúracha go deo

115. **The oldest sister**
An deirfiúr is sine

116. **The middle sister**
An deirfiúr i lár báire

117. **The youngest sister**
An deirfiúr is óige

118. **My sister, my friend**
Mo dheirfiúr, mo chara

119. **My sister, my friend** *(voc.)*
A dheirfiúr, a chara

120. **My sister, my best friend**
Mo dheirfiúr, cara mo chléibh *(lit. My sister, my bosom friend)*
Mo dheirfiúr, mo dhlúthchara *(lit. My sister, my close friend)*

121. **My sister, my best friend** *(voc.)*
A dheirfiúr, a chara mo chléibh
A dheirfiúr, a dhlúthchara

122. **Son**
Mac

123. **My son**
Mo mhac

124. **My son** *(voc.)*
A mhic

125. **My sons** *or* **My boys**
Mo chlann mhac

126. **My handsome son**
Mo mhac dóighiúil

127. **Two handsome sons**
Beirt mhac dóighiúil

128. **Three handsome sons**
Triúr mac dóighiúil

129. **Four handsome sons**
Ceathrar mac dóighiúil

130. **A son like his mother and a daughter like her father**
Mac mar a mháthair agus iníon mar a hathair

Love and friendship

131.   **I am my beloved's and my beloved is mine** *(Song of Songs/Song of Solomon 6:3, direct quote from* An Bíobla Naofa; *genders of both the lover and the beloved are unspecified)*
Le mo ghrása mise, agus liomsa mo ghrá

132.   **My beloved is mine and I am his** *(Song of Songs/Song of Solomon 2:16, direct quote from* An Bíobla Naofa; *beloved is male, speaker is non-gender-specific)*
Liomsa mo ghrá agus leis-sean mise

133.   **My beloved is mine and I am hers** *(paraphrase of Song of Songs/Song of Solomon 2:16; beloved is female; speaker is non-gender-specific)*
Liomsa mo ghrá agus léise mise

134.   **Eternal love**
Grá go buan
Buanghrá

135.   **Eternally**
Go buan
Go síoraí

136.   **Everlasting**
Buan
Síor
Seasmhach

137.   **Forever**
Go brách
Go deo

138.   **Forever and ever**
Go deo na ndeor
Go brách na breithe

139. **Friend**
Cara

140. **Friends**
Cairde

141. **Friends forever**
Cairde go brách
Cairde go deo
Buanchairde

142. **My friend**
Mo chara

143. **My friend** *(voc.)*
A chara

144. **My best friend**
Mo dhlúthchara *(lit. My compact or close friend)*
Cara mo chléibh *(lit. My bosom friend)*

145. **My best friend** *(voc.)*
A dhlúthchara *(lit. My compact or close friend)*
A chara mo chléibh *(lit. My compact/close friend)*

146. **Friendship**
Cairdeas

147. **Friendship and love**
Cairdeas is grá

148. **Friendship, love, loyalty**
Cairdeas, grá, dílseacht

149. **Husband**
Fear céile

150. **My husband**
M'fhear céile

151. **My dear husband** *or* **My beloved husband**
M'fhear céile dil

152. **Husband and wife**
Fear is bean

153. **Love** *(noun; refers only to love for other living beings)*
Grá
Searc

154. **My love** *or* **My beloved**
Mo ghrá *(if speaking about your beloved)*
A ghrá *(voc.)*

155. **For my love's sake**
Ar son mo ghrá

156. **My lover** *(romantic term; does not imply an extra-marital relationship)*
Mo leannán

157. **I love you** *(sing., said to one person)*
Tá grá agam duit *(lit. I have love for you)*
Mo ghrá thú *(lit. You are my love)*
Grá mo chroí thú *(lit. You are the love of my heart)*
Tá mo chroí istigh ionat *(lit. My heart is within you* or *You have my heart)*

158. **I love you** *(pl., said to multiple people)*
Tá grá agam daoibh *(lit. I have love for you)*
Mo ghrá sibh *(lit. You are my love)*
Grá mo chroí sibh *(lit. You are the love of my heart)*
Tá mo chroí istigh ionaibh *(lit. My heart is within you* or *You have my heart)*

159. **Love is patient, love is kind** *(1 Corinthians 13:4)*
Bíonn an grá foighneach agus bíonn sé lách

160. **Love never fails** *(1 Corinthians 13:8)*
Ní rachaidh an grá i léig go deo

161. **Therefore faith, hope, and love abide, these three, but the greatest of these is love** *(1 Corinthians 13:13)*
Tá trí nithe ann atá buan, más ea, creideamh, dóchas agus grá, ach is é an grá an ní is mó.

162. **The greatest of these is love** *(1 Corinthians 13:13, final phrase)*
Is é an grá an ní is mó *(direct quote)*
Is é an grá an ní ba mhó acu *(paraphrase: Love is the greatest of these)*

163. **My partner** *or* **My spouse** *(not gender-specific)*
Mo chéile

164. **Soulmate** *or* **Soul friend** *(platonic friendship; see Chapter 3)*
Cara anama *(lit. Soul friend)*
Buanchara *(lit. Eternal friend)*
Dlúthchara *(lit. Close or compact friend)*

165. **My soulmate** *or* **My soul friend** *(platonic friendship; see Chapter 3)*
Cara m'anama/A chara m'anama *(voc.)*
Mo bhuanchara/A bhuanchara *(voc.)*
Mo dhlúthchara/A dhlúthchara *(voc.)*

166. **Soulmates** *or* **Soul friends** *(platonic friendship; see Chapter 3)*
Cairde anama *(lit. Soul friends)*
Buanchairde *(lit. Eternal friends)*
Dlúthchairde *(lit. Close or compact friends)*

167. **Soulmate** *(romantic; see Chapter 3)*
Buanghrá *(lit. Eternal love)*
Céadsearc *(lit. First love, as in original/primary love)*
Síorghrá** *(lit. Eternal love)*
Fíorghrá** *(lit. True love)*
Sonuachar *(lit. True/good spouse)*

168. **My soulmate** *(romantic; see discussion in Chapter 3)*
Mo bhuanghrá *or* A bhuanghrá *(voc.; lit. O my eternal love)*
Mo chéadsearc *or* A chéadsearc *(voc.; lit. O my first [original/primary] love)*
Mo shíorghrá *or* A shíorghrá** *(voc.; lit. O my eternal love)*
M'fhíorghrá *or* A fhíorghrá** *(voc.; lit. O my true love)*
Mo shonuachar *or* A shonuachar *(voc.; lit. O my true/ good spouse)*

169. **Terms of endearment** *(All the terms of endearment below can be translated into English as "my darling," "my love," or "my sweetheart." They would not generally be translated literally. Literal meanings are given simply for interest. All terms are in the vocative case, i.e., as if they were being spoken directly to someone rather than about that person).*
A chéadsearc *(lit. O first/original love; typically reserved for romantic love)*
A chuisle *(lit. O pulse)*
A chuisle mo chroí *(lit. O pulse of my heart)*
A chumann *(lit. O darling; generally reserved for romantic love)*
A ghrá *(lit. O love/beloved)*
A ghrá geal *(lit. O bright/shining love)*
A ghrá mo chroí *(lit. O love of my heart)*
A mhuirnín *(lit. O darling)*
A rún *(lit. O secret)*
A stór *(lit. O treasure)*
A stóirín *(lit. O little treasure)*
A thaisce *(lit. O treasure; frequently used for, but not limited to, children)*

170. **Wife**
Bean chéile

171. **My wife**
Mo bhean chéile

172. **My dear wife** *or* **My beloved wife**
Mo bhean chéile dhil

173. **What God has joined together, let no one put asunder** *(Bible, Mark 10:9)*
An ní a cheangail Dia, ná scaoileadh duine é

In memoriam

174. **Broken-hearted**
Croíbhriste

175. **My heart is broken**
Tá mo chroí briste

176. **Our hearts are broken**
Tá ár gcroí briste

177. **Eternal rest to her**
Suaimhneas síoraí uirthi

178. **Eternal rest to him**
Suaimhneas síoraí air

179. **Eternal rest to them**
Suaimhneas síoraí orthu

180. **Eternal rest to you**
Suaimhneas síoraí ort *(sing.)*
Suaimhneas síoraí oraibh *(pl.)*

181. **I miss you**
Tá cumha orm i do dhiaidh *(sing.)*
Tá cumha orm in bhur ndiaidh *(pl.)*
Airím uaim thú *(sing.)*
Airím uaim sibh *(pl.)*

182. **May God hold you in the palm of his hand**
Go gcoinní Dia i mbois a láimhe thú *(sing.)*
Go gcoinní Dia i mbois a láimhe sibh *(pl.)*

183. **May her soul be at God's right hand**
Ar dheis Dé go raibh a hanam

184. **May his soul be at God's right hand**
Ar dheis Dé go raibh a anam

185. **May their souls be at God's right hand**
Ar dheis Dé go raibh a n-anam

186. **May your soul be at God's right hand**
Ar dheis Dé go raibh d'anam *(sing.)*
Ar dheis Dé go raibh bhur n-anam *(pl.)*

187. **He has departed on the way of truth** *(traditional saying when someone has died)*
Tá sé imithe ar shlí na fírinne

188. **He is in the midst of the angels**
Tá sé i measc na n-aingeal

189. **In loving memory**
I ndilchuimhne

190. **In the arms of the angels**
I lámha na n-aingeal

191. **She is in the midst of the angels**
Tá sí i measc na n-angeal

192. **She has departed on the way of truth** *(traditional saying when someone has died)*
Tá sí imithe ar shlí na fírinne

193. **They are in the midst of the angels**
Tá siad i measc na n-aingeal

194. **They have departed on the way of truth**
Tá siad imithe ar shlí na fírinne

195. **Until we meet again**
Go gcastar le chéile sinn arís *(direct translation from "An Irish Blessing")*

196. **We miss you**
Tá cumha orainn i do dhiaidh *(sing.)*
Tá cumha orainn in bhur ndiaidh *(pl.)*
Airímid uainn thú
Airíonn muid uainn thú
Airímid uainn sibh
Airíonn muid uainn sibh

197. **You are in my heart forever** (*lit. You will be in my heart forever*)
Beidh tú i mo chroí go brách *(sing.)*
Beidh tú i mo chroí go deo *(sing.)*
Beidh sibh i mo chroí go brách *(pl.)*
Beidh sibh i mo chroí go deo *(pl.)*

Religious and spiritual

198. **Air, earth, fire, water**
Aer, talamh, tine, uisce

199. **Angel**
Aingeal

200. **Angels**
Aingil

201. **Angels and demons**
Aingil is deamhain

202. **An it harm none, do what ye will** (*Wiccan Rede; archaic English*)
Mura ndéantar dochar do dhuine eile, déan mar is toil leat féin *(sing.)*
Mura ndéantar dochar do dhuine eile, déanaigí mar is toil libh féin *(pl.)*

203. **As above, so below**
Thíos mar atá thuas *(lit. Below as it is above)*

204. **Be still and know that I am God** *(Bible, Psalm 46:11)*
Éistigí! Bíodh a fhios agaibh gur mise is Dia ann *(pl.; lit. "Listen/Hear! Know that I am God." Direct quote from* An Bíobla Naofa*)*
Éist! Bíodh a fhios agat gur mise is Dia ann *(sing.; paraphrase, said to one person)*

205. **Blessed**
Beannaithe

206. **Blessing**
Beannacht

207. **Blessed be** *(lit. A blessing on you)*
Beannacht ort *(sing.)*
Beannacht oraibh *(pl.)*

208. **Christ be with me** *(St. Patrick's Breastplate)*

Christ with me, Christ before me
Críost liom, Críost romham

Christ behind me, Christ within me
Críost i mo dhiaidh, Críost istigh ionam

Christ beneath me, Christ above me
Críost fúm, Críost os mo chionn

Christ on my right hand, Christ on my left hand
Críost ar mo lámh dheas, Críost ar mo lámh chlé

Christ in my lying, Christ in my standing (or Christ when I'm asleep and Christ when I'm awake),
Críost i mo luí dom, Críost i mo sheasamh dom

Christ in the heart of all who know me
Críost i gcroí gach duine atá ag cuimhneamh orm

Christ in the mouth of all who speak to me
Críost i mbéal gach duine a labhraíonn liom
(continued on next page)

Christ in every eye that sees me
Críost i ngach súil a fhéachann orm

Christ in every ear that hears me
Críost i ngach cluais a éisteann liom

209. **Crone**
Cailleach feasa

210. **The Devil**
An Diabhal

211. **Devils**
Diabhail

212. **Druid**
Draoi

213. **Female druid**
Bandraoi

214. **Christian (noun)**
Críostaí

215. **Everlasting life**
An bheatha shíoraí

216. **Evil**
Olc

217. **Faith** *(religious belief)*
Creideamh

218. **Father**
Athair

219. **Father, Son, Holy Spirit**
Athair, Mac, Spiorad Naomh

220. **The Father, the Son, and the Holy Spirit**
An tAthair, an Mac, agus an Spiorad Naomh

221. **In the name of the Father, and of the Son, and of the Holy Spirit**
In ainm an Athar, agus an Mhic, agus an Spioraid Naoimh

222. **Fate**
Cinniúint

223. **God**
Dia

224. **Gods**
Déithe

225. **The gods**
Na déithe

226. **Goddess**
Bandia

227. **Goddesses**
Bandéithe

228. **Good and evil**
Maith agus olc
Maitheas agus olc

229. **Goodness**
Maith
Maitheas

230. **Grace**
Grásta

231. **The grace of God** *or* **God's grace**
Grásta Dé

232. **By the grace of God**
Le grásta Dé

233. **You are saved by grace, through faith** *(Bible, Ephesians 2:8)*
Is le grásta a slánaíodh sibh, trí chreideamh *(pl., direct quote from* An Bíobla Naofa*)*
Is le grásta a slánaíodh tú, trí chreideamh *(sing.; paraphrase)*

234. **Heaven**
Neamh
Na Flaithis *(poetic: lit. The Principalities)*

235. **Hell**
Ifreann

236. **Holy** *or* **Sacred** *(adj.)*
Naofa

237. **The Holy Spirit**
An Spiorad Naomh

238. **The Holy Trinity**
An Tríonóid Naofa

239. **I can do all things through Christ who strengthens me** *(Bible, Philippians 4:13)*
Táim in ann gach ní a dhéanamh le cabhair an té úd a thugann neart dom *(direct translation from* An Bíobla Naofa*; lit. I am able to do everything with the help of the one who gives me strength; Christ is implied, but not specifically mentioned.)*

240. **Jesus**
Íosa

241. **Jesus Christ**
Íosa Críost

242. **Jesus, Mary, Joseph**
Íosa, Muire, Seosamh

243. **Jesus, Mary, Joseph** *(voc.)*
A Íosa, A Mhuire, A Sheosaimh

244. **Saint Joseph**
Naomh Seosamh

245. **The Lord**
An Tiarna

246. **May the Lord be with you**
Go raibh an Tiarna leat *(sing.)*
Go raibh an Tiarna libh *(pl.)*

247. **The Lord's Prayer** *or* **The Our Father** *(line by line)*

Our father who art in Heaven
Ár nAthair atá ar Neamh

Hallowed be thy name
Go naofar d'ainm

Thy kingdom come
Go dtaga do ríocht

Thy will be done
Go ndéantar do thoil

On Earth as it is in Heaven
Ar an Talamh mar atá ar Neamh
Ar an Talamh mar a dhéantar ar Neamh *(either of these forms can be used)*

Give us this day our daily bread
Ár n-arán laethúil tabhair dúinn inniu

And forgive us our sins
Agus maith dúinn ár bhfiacha

As we forgive those who sin against us
Mar a mhaithimidne dár bhféichiúnaithe féin

And lead us not into temptation
Agus ná lig sinn i gcathú
(continued on next page)

But deliver us from evil
Ach saor sinn ó olc

For thine is the kingdom and the power and the glory
Óir is leatsa an ríocht agus an chumhacht agus an ghlóir

Forever and ever, amen
Trí shaol na saol. Áiméan.

248. **Magic**
Draíocht

249. **Maiden**
Maighdean

250. **Mary**
Muire *(mother of Jesus only; note that the Irish name for all other women named "Mary" is "Máire")*

251. **The Blessed Virgin**
An Mhaighdean Bheannaithe

252. **The Virgin Mary**
An Mhaighdean Mhuire

253. **Mercy**
Trócaire

254. **Lord have mercy**
A Thiarna déan trócaire

255. **Merry meet and merry part and merry meet again**
Sona do theacht agus sona d'imeacht agus sona do theacht arís *(sing.; to omit the second half, "and merry meet again," omit "agus sona do theacht arís")*
Sona bhur dteacht agus sona bhur n-imeacht agus sona bhur dteacht arís *(pl.; to omit the second half, "and merry meet again," omit "agus sona bhur dteacht arís")*

256. **Pagan**
Páganach

257. **Paradise**
Parthas

258. **Psalm 23** *(line-by-line)*

The Lord is my shepherd
Is é an Tiarna m'aoire

I shall not want
Ní bheidh aon ní de dhíth orm

He makes me lie down in green pastures
Cuireann sé féin i mo luí mé i móinéar féir ghlais

He leads me beside still waters. He restores my soul
Seolann sé ar imeall an uisce mé mar a bhfaighim
suaimhneas *(lit. He leads me on the brink of the water,
that I may find rest)*

He leads me in the paths of righteousness
Seolann sé ar shlí na fíréantachta mé

For his name's sake
mar gheall ar a ainm

*Though I walk through the valley of the shadow of
death*
Fiú dá siúlfainn i ngleann an dorchadais *(lit. Though I
walk through the valley of darkness)*

I will fear no evil
níor bhaol liom an t-olc *(lit. Evil will not threaten me)*

Your rod and your staff, they comfort me
Agus tú faram le do shlat is do bhachall chun sólás a
thabhairt dom *(lit. And you before me with your rod
and your staff to give me solace)*

You prepare a table for me in the presence of my enemies
Cóiríonn tú bord chun béile dom i láthair mo naimhde
(continued on next page)

You have annointed my head with oil
Ungann tú mo cheann le hola (*lit. You anoint my head with oil*)

My cup overflows
Tá mo chupa ag cur thairis

Goodness and mercy shall follow me all the days of my life
Leanfaidh cineáltas is buanghrá mé gach lá de mo shaol (*lit. Kindness and eternal love will follow me every day of my life*)

I will dwell in the house of the Lord forever
I dteach an Tiarna a mhairfidh mé go brách na breithe

259. **So mote it be** (*So may it be, in archaic English*)
Go raibh sé amhlaidh (*lit. May it be so*)

260. **Sinner**
Peacach

261. **Salvation**
Slánú

262. **Saved**
Slánaithe

263. **Saviour**
Slánaitheoir

264. **My Saviour**
Mo Shlánaitheoir

265. **My Saviour** (*voc.*)
A Shlánaitheoir

266. **Band of brothers**
Buíon bráithre

267. **Brotherhood**
Bráithreachas
An Bráithreachas *(lit. The Brotherhood)*

268. **Bravery**
Crógacht

269. **Clear the way!** *or* **Out of the way!** *(battle cry of New York's Fighting 69th Regiment and of the Enniskillin Fusiliers)*
Fág an bealach!

270. **Conqueror** *or* **Victor**
Buaiteoir
Cathbhuach *(lit. one who is victorious in battle)*

271. **Courage**
Misneach

272. **Death before dishonour**
An bás níos túisce ná an easonóir *(lit. Death in preference to dishonour)*

273. **Death from above** *(Airborne motto)*
An bás anuas *(lit. Death from above)*
An bás ón spéir anuas *(lit. Death coming down from the sky)*

274. **Follow me** *(U.S. Army Infantry motto)*
Lean mise *(sing.)*
Leanaigí mise *(pl.)*

275. **The heart of a hero**
Croí an laoich

276. **The heart of a warrior**
Croí an ghaiscígh

277. **Hero**
Laoch

278. **My hero**
Mo laoch

279. **Heroes**
Laochra

280. **My heroes**
Mo laochra

281. **Heroine**
Banlaoch

282. **My heroine**
Mo bhanlaoch

283. **Heroines**
Banlaochra

284. **My heroines**
Mo bhanlaochra

285. **Honour**
Onóir

286. **Keep the peace** *(imperative)*
Coimeád an tsíocháin *(sing.)*
Coimeádaigí an tsíocháin *(pl.)*

287. **Patriot****
Tírghráthóir

288. **Patriotism****
Tírghrá

289. **To protect and to serve**
Cosaint agus fónamh *(lit. Protection and service)*

290. **Semper Fidelis** *(Always Faithful; U.S. Marine Corps motto)*
Dílis go deo *(lit. Faithful forever)*
Dílis go brách *(lit. Faithful forever)*
Dílis i gcónaí *(lit. Faithful at all times/constantly)*
Bithdhílis *(lit. Constantly and eternally faithful)*

291. **Soldier**
Saighdiúir

292. **My soldier**
Mo shaighdiúir

293. **Soldiers**
Saighdiúirí

294. **My soldiers**
Mo shaighdiúirí

295. **Victory**
Bua

296. **Victory or death**
Bua nó bás

297. **Warrior**
Gaiscíoch

298. **My warrior**
Mo ghaiscíoch

299. **Warriors**
Gaiscígh

300. **My warriors**
Mo ghaiscígh

301. **Who never fled from the clash of swords** *(Motto of New York's Fighting 69th Regiment)*
Riamh nár dhruid ó spairn lann

Work, activities, and identities

302. **Actor**
Aisteoir

303. **Artist**
Ealaíontóir

304. **Athlete**
Lúthchleasaí

305. **Bookworm** *or* **Avid reader**
Léitheoir craosach

306. **Dance** *(noun)*
Rince
Damhsa

307. **Dancer**
Rinceoir
Damhsóir

308. **Doctor**
Dochtúir

309. **Fiddler**
Fidléir

310. **Firefighter**
Fear dóiteáin *or* Fear tine *(fireman)*
Bean dhóiteáin *or* Bean tine *(firewoman)*
Duine múchta dóiteáin** *(non-gender-specific; lit. A person who extinguishes fires)*

311. **Fisherman**
Iascaire

312. **Gambler**
Cearrbhach

313. **Harper** *or* **Harpist**
Cláirseoir
Cruitire

314. **Healer**
Lia
Leigheasóir**

315. **Hunter**
Sealgaire

316. **Mermaid** *or* **Selkie**
Murúch *(female or male)*
Maighdean mhara *(female only)*

317. **Music**
Ceol

318. **Musician**
Ceoltóir

319. **Nurse** *(female)*
Banaltra

320. **Nurse** *(male)*
Altra fir

321. **Piper**
Píobaire

322. **Pirate**
Foghlaí mara

323. **Poet**
File

324. **Professor**
Ollamh

325. **Sailor**
Mairnéalach

326. **Singer**
Amhránaí

327. **Teacher**
Múinteoir

328. **Vegetarian**
Feoilséantóir

Emotions, qualities, and concepts

329. **Alive** *(adj.)*
Beo

330. **Beautiful**
Álainn

331. **Beauty**
Áilleacht

332. **Bliss**
Aoibhneas

333. **Blissful**
Aoibhinn

334. **Bravery**
Crógacht

335. **Brave** *(adj.)*
Cróga

336. **Confidence**
Muinín

337. **Confident**
Muiníneach

338. **Courage**
Misneach

339. **Courageous** *or* **Brave**
Misniúil

340. **Free** *(as in "free from bondage")*
Saor

341. **Freedom**
Saoirse

342. **Happiness**
Sonas
Gliondar

343. **Happy**
Sona
Gliondrach

344. **Hatred**
Fuath
Gráin

345. **Healing** *(noun)*
Leigheas

346. **Hope**
Dóchas

347. **Hopeful**
Dóchasach

348. **Infinity** *(noun)*
Dochuimseacht
Éigríoch

349. **Infinite** *(adj.)*
Gan chuimse gan teorainn *(lit. Without limits without boundaries)*

350. **Joy**
Áthas

351. **Joyful**
Áthasach

352. **Life**
Beatha

353. **Luck**
Ádh

354. **Good luck to you**
Ádh mór ort *(sing.)*
Ádh mór oraibh *(pl.)*

355. **Lucky**
Ámharach

356. **Laughter**
Gáire

357. **Mighty**
Neartmhar

358. **Peace** *(absence of conflict)*
Síocháin

359. **Peace** *(tranquility)*
Suaimhneas

360. **Power**
Cumhacht

361. **Powerful**
Cumhachtach

362. **Pride**
Bród

363. **Prosperity**
Rath

364. **Proud**
Bródúil

365. **Sacrifice** *(noun)*
Íobairt

366. **Strength**
Neart

367. **Strong**
Láidir

368. **Success**
Rath

Personal mottos and sayings

369. **Dance as if no one is watching**
Déan damhsa amhail is nach bhfuil éinne ag féachaint *(sing.)*
Déanagaí damhsa amhail is nach bhfuil éinne ag féachaint *(pl.)*

370. **Don't forget to breathe**
Ná déan dearmad anáil a tharraingt *(sing.)*
Ná déanaigí dearmad anáil a tharraingt *(pl.)*

371. **Dream as if you will live forever; live as if you will die today**
Déan do chuid aislingí amhail is go mairfidh tú go deo agus mair amhail is gur inniu do lá deireanach ar an saol *(sing., lit. Dream as if you will live forever and live as if today where your last day of life)*

372. **Drug-free**
Saor ó dhrugaí *(lit. Free of drugs or Free from drugs)*

373. **Everything happens for a reason**
Tá cúis le gach rud a tharlaíonn *(lit. There is a reason for everything that happens)*

374. **Hold your ground** *or* **Stand your ground**
Seas an fód *(sing.)*
Seasaigí an fód *(pl.)*

375. **He flies with his own wings** *(see entry 391)*
Lena chuid sciathán féin a eitlíonn sé

376. **He walks alone**
Siúlann sé ina aonar

377. **I am myself**
Is mise mé féin

378. **Love as if you've never been hurt**
Tabhair grá amhail is nár gortaíodh riamh thú *(sing.)*
Tugaigí grá amhail is nár gortaíodh riamh sibh *(pl.)*

379. **Live every day as if it were your last**
Caith gach lá amhail is gurb é an lá deireanach agat é *(sing.)*
Caithigí gach lá amhail is gurb é an lá deireanach agaibh é *(pl.)*
Gach lá mar an lá deiridh *(lit. Every day like the last day)*

380. **Live, laugh, love**
Beatha, gáire, grá *(lit. Life, laughter, love; nouns work better than verbs here)*

381. **Live life to the fullest**
Bain ceol as an saol *(sing., lit. Reap music from life)*
Bainigí ceol as an saol *(pl., lit. Reap music from life)*
Bain sult as an saol *(sing., lit. Reap pleasure from life)*
Bainigí sult as an saol *(pl., lit. Reap pleasure from life)*

382. **Live to ride; ride to live**
Bí beo ag marcaíocht; bí ag marcaíocht le bheith beo** *(sing., lit. Be alive for riding; ride to be alive)*
Bígí beo ag marcaíocht; bígí ag marcaíocht le bheith beo** *(pl., lit. Be alive for riding; ride to be alive)*
Ní beo go marcaíocht agus ní marcaíocht go beo *(lit. There is no living without riding and no riding without living)*

383. **Music heals the broken soul**
Leigheasann an ceol an t-anam briste
Is leigheas é an ceol ar an anam briste *(lit. Music is the healer of the broken soul)*

384. **My Irish eyes are smiling**
Tá loinnir i mo shúile Gaelacha *(lit. There is a gleam in my Irish eyes)*

385. **My Irish eyes are always smiling**
Bíonn loinnir i mo shúile Gaelacha i gcónaí

386. **Nevertheless, she persisted**
Ina ainneoin sin, lean sí ar aghaidh *(lit. In spite of that, she persisted)*

387. **No fear**
Gan eagla *(lit. Without fear)*
Gan faitíos *(lit. Without fear)*
Gan scáth gan eagla *(Without any fear whatsoever, lit. Without a shadow without fear; Irish may use a list of words to indicate intensity or comprehensiveness where English would use an expression like "whatsoever")*

388. **No regret** *or* **No regrets**
Gan aiféala *(lit. without regret/no regrets)*
Níl aiféala ar bith orm *(lit. I have no regrets)*
Gan chreach gan mhairg *(lit. without hindrance or troubles)*

389. **Only God can judge me**
Tús na breithe ag Dia *(lit. Judgement originates with God, also translated as God is our principal judge; this is the most Irish-sounding choice)*
Is ag Dia amháin atá cead breithiúnas a thabhairt orm *(lit. God alone has the permission or right to judge me)*
Is é Dia amháin a thabharfaidh breithiúnas orm *(lit. Only God will judge me or God alone will judge me)*

390. **Seize the day** *or* **Carpe diem**
Tapaigh do dheis *(lit. Grasp or take hold of your opportunity, sing.)*
Tapaígí an deis *(pl.)*

391. **She flies with her own wings** *(English version of the Latin motto of the U.S. state of Oregon,* Alis volat propriis, *[One] flies with [one's] own wings)*
Lena cuid sciathán féin a eitlíonn sí

392. **She walks alone**
Siúlann sí ina haonar

393. **Sing as if no one is listening**
Abair amhrán amhail is nach bhfuil éinne ag éisteacht *(sing.)*
Abraígí amhrán amhail is nach bhfuil éinne ag éisteacht *(pl.)*

394. **Take it easy**
Tóg go bog é *(sing.)*
Tógaigí go bog é *(pl.)*
Tóg go réidh é *(sing.)*
Tógaigí go réidh é *(pl.)*

395. **That which does not kill me makes me stronger**
An rud nach maraíonn mé neartaíonn sé mé

396. **This too shall pass**
Imeoidh sé seo leis *(Munster)*
Imeoidh sé seo freisin *(Connacht)*
Imeoidh sé seo fosta *(Ulster)*

397. **What goes around comes around**
Filleann an feall ar an bhfeallaire *(Irish saying, lit. Treachery returns to the traitor)*

398. **When Irish eyes are smiling**
Nuair a bhíonn loinnir i súile an Ghaeil *(When there is a gleam in the eyes of an Irish person)*

399. **When Irish eyes are smiling they're usually up to something**
Nuair atá loinnir i súile na nGael, is iondúil rud sa treis acu

400. **YOLO** *(You only live once)*
Níl agat ach an t-aon saol amháin *(lit. You only have one life)*
Bí beo le do bheo *(lit. Be alive while you live)*

Quotes from movies, TV, and literature

401. **Aequitas – Veritas** *(Justice – Truth, from "Boondock Saints")*
An Chóir – An Ceart
Ceart agus Cóir *(lit. Truth and Justice)*

402. **The girl made lovely by sorrow**** *(see Chapter 3; paraphrased from the poem "An tAmhránaí" by Louis de Paor)*
An cailín a bhfuil áilleacht an bhróin ina gnúis *(lit. The girl with the beauty of sorrow in her face; this is the actual line from the poem)*
An cailín ar chuir an brón áilleacht inti** *(lit. The girl that sorrow has made beautiful; paraphrase)*

403. **Live long and prosper** *(from "Star Trek")*
Saol fada faoi rath ort *(sing.)*
Saol fada faoi rath oraibh *(pl.)*

404. **May the Force be with you** *(from "Star Wars")*
Go raibh an Fórsa leat *(sing.)*
Go raibh an Fórsa libh *(pl.)*

405. **The needs of the many outweigh the needs of the few**
(from "Star Trek")
Is tábhachtaí riar an mhóráin ná riar an bheagáin *(lit. The needs of the many are more important than the needs of the few)*

406. **Never shall innocent blood be shed, but the blood of the wicked shall flow like a river** *(from "Boondock Saints")*
Ní dhoirtfear fuil dhaoine gan urchóid ach rithfidh fuil lucht an oilc ina tuilte.

407. **Not all those who wander are lost** *(from J.R.R Tolkien, The Lord of the Rings)*
Ní bhíonn gach fánaí ar strae *(lit. Not every wanderer is lost)*

408. **A prayer for the wild at heart [that are] kept in cages**
(from a poem by Tennessee Williams)
Paidir dóibhsean le fíantas ina gcroí atá coinnithe i gcaighin

409. **And shepherds we shall be, for thee, my Lord, for thee** *(from "Boondock Saints")*
Agus beimid inár n-aoirí ar do shonsa, a Thiarna, ar do shonsa

Traditional Irish sayings and proverbs (seanfhocail)

410. **A country without a language is a country without a soul**
Tír gan teanga, tír gan anam

411. **A friend is known in hardship**
Aithnítear cara i gcruatan

412. **A good run is better than a bad stand**
Is fearr rith maith ná drochsheasamh

413. **A good name is better than riches**
Is fearr clú ná conách

414. **A light heart lives long**
Maireann croí éadrom i bhfad

415. **A word is more enduring than worldy wealth**
Is buaine focal ná toice an tsaoil

416. **God's help is closer than the door**
Is gaire cabhair Dé ná an doras

417. **Health is better than wealth**
Is fearr an tsláinte ná na táinte

418. **Irish Blessing** *(line-by-line; the famous first line is actually a mistranslation into English based on a misunderstanding of the Irish idiom)*

    May the road rise up to meet you
    Go n-éirí an bóthar leat
    (lit. May your road or journey be successful)

    May the wind be always at your back
    Go raibh cóir na gaoithe i gcónaí leat
    (lit. May a fair wind be always with you)
    (continued on next page)

May the sun shine warm upon your face
Go dtaitní an ghrian go bog tláith ar chlár d'éadain
(lit. May the sun shine softly on your forehead)

May the rain fall soft upon your fields
Go dtite an bháisteach go bog mín ar do chuid talún

And until we meet again
Agus go gcastar le chéile sinn arís

May God hold you in the hollow of his hand
Go gcoinní Dia i mbois a láimhe thú

419. **It is not always the great men who reap the harvest**
Ní hiad na fir mhóra amháin a bhaineas an fómhar

420. **May you be a half hour in Heaven before the devil knows you're dead**
Go raibh tú leathuair ar neamh sula mbíonn a fhios ag an diabhal go bhfuil tú marbh *(sing.)*
Go raibh sibh leathuair ar neamh sula mbíonn a fhios ag an diabhal go bhfuil sibh marbh *(pl.)*

421. **No matter how long the day is, the evening comes**
Dá fhaid an lá, tagann an tráthnóna

422. **No man is an island**
Maireann na daoine ar scáth a chéile *(lit. People live in one another's shadow)*

423. **Say little but say it well**
Beagán a rá agus é a rá go maith

424. **The Chant of the Fianna** *(or Dord na Féinne; line-by-line)*

Laughter in our hearts
Gaire inár gcroí

Strength in our limbs
Neart inár ngéaga

Deeds according to our word
Beart de réir ár mbriathar

425. **There is many a twist in life**
Is iomaí cor sa saol

426. **There's no place like home**
Níl aon tinteán mar do thinteán féin *(lit. There is no fireside like your own fireside)*

427. **There is no strength without unity**
Ní neart go cur le chéile

428. **The person who is not strong had better be clever**
An té nach bhfuil láidir ní folá dó a bheith glic

429. **The work praises the man**
Molann an obair an fear

430. **When the wine is in(side), the sense is out(side)** *(In vino veritas)*
Nuair a bhíonn an fíon istigh, bíonn an chiall amuigh

Resources

Translation assistance and verification

Letters and Numbers, Ltd. / Aakkoset ja Numerot Oy
aakkosetjanumerot.com/translation/
info@aakkosetjanumerot.com
This Finland-based translation service, owned and operated by a fluent Irish speaker, has recently added "English-Irish" to its translation options.

Irish Translators' and Interpreters' Association
(*Cumann Aistritheoirí agus Teangairí na hÉireann*)
www.translatorsassociation.ie
Maintains lists of qualified professional translators to and from various languages, including English-Irish.

The Irish Language Forum (ILF)
www.irishlanguageforum.com
Offers free, human translations and translation confirmation on its main forum, *An Fóram Mór*. ILF also provides support and community for people who are learning Irish and Scottish Gaelic. Registration is required.

Pronunciation assistance

Teanglann.ie Pronunciation Database
www.teanglann.ie/en/fuaim/
Allows you to hear individual words spoken in each of the three main dialects of Irish. Type the word you want (including accent marks) in the search box and click on the dialect desired. Does not accommodate full phrases.

Abair
www.abair.ie
A project of Trinity College, Dublin, Abair.ie allows you to hear words and phrases pronounced in the three main dialects of Irish and some sub-

dialects. The site is in Irish, but easy to use: choose the dialect you want, type the word or phrase you want in the search box, and click on "*Déan Sintéis.*" While this program can accommodate full phrases, it generally does better with individual words.

Forvo
www.forvo.com
Irish is one of the languages supported by Forvo. Recordings are made by live people rather than synthesized. You can listen to already-recorded pronunciations without registering, but you must register (free) to request a word or phrase. As Forvo doesn't restrict who can provide pronunciations, it's important to choose something made by a native speaker, if possible.

Writing and scripts

Information about *Seanchló/Cló Gaelach*, a traditional Irish form of the Latin alphabet:
www.omniglot.com/writing/clogaelach.htm

Information about Ogham, an ancient writing system:
www.omniglot.com/writing/ogham.htm

Gaelchlo
www.gaelchlo.com
A source of traditional and modern Irish fonts available for free download. The site is in Irish, but is easy to use by following these instructions:
1. Click on "Clónna" at the top of the page. You'll be taken to a page with examples of all the fonts available for download.
2. Click on the font you want. You'll be taken to a page about that font.
3. Some of the fonts can be downloaded directly from the font's page. Scroll down to the bottom of the page. If you see a link with a ".zip" file extension, you can download the font directly. Save it in your word processor's "fonts" folder, and you're ready to go.
4. If you don't see a .zip file, you'll need to send an email with the name of the font in the title to post@gaelchlo.com.

"Are You a Fada-less Child?", The Geeky Gaeilgeoir
Learn how to type the *síneadh fada* (acute accent mark) on any computer, smartphone, or tablet. See archive at:
www.audreynickel.com

Irish language learning resources

"Beyond Duolingo," The Geeky Gaeilgeoir
Information on free and low-cost Irish self-teaching programs and other resources. Regularly updated. See archive at:
www.audreynickel.com

Recommended reading

Ní Chartúir, Darerca, *The Irish Language: An Overview and Guide.* New York, Avena Press, 2002.
History, development, and status of the Irish language, including basic information about studying the language.

Eco, Umberto, *Mouse or Rat? Translation as Negotiation.* Phoenix (an imprint of Orion Publishing, Ltd.), 2004.
An in-depth look at the challenges of translating from one language to another.

Glossary Index

A

above 66, 203, 208, 273
actor 302
aequitas 401
air 198
Airborne 273
alive 329, 382, 400
all 66, 407
alone 376, 389, 392
always 290, 385, 418, 419
amen 247
America 19
American 11
angel 199
angels 188, 190, 191,193, 200,
        201
annointed 258
Army 274
around 397
artist 303
athlete 304

B

baby 26, 27, 28, 29
beautiful 61, 62, 63, 64, 330
beauty 331
beloved 34, 74, 89, 101, 113,
        131, 132, 133, 151, 154,
        169, 172
below 203
best 41, 42, 120, 121, 144, 145
birth 15
blessed 205, 207, 251

blessing 195, 481
bliss 332
blissful 333
blood 406
book-lover 305
bookworm 305
Boondock Saints 401, 406, 409
boy 12
boys 125
brave 335, 339
bravery 268, 334
bread 247
breastplate 208
breathe 370
bright 169
broken 174, 175, 176, 383
broken-hearted 174
brother 30, 31, 32, 33, 34, 35,
        36, 37, 38, 39, 40, 41, 42
brothers 31, 35, 266
brotherhood 267

C

cages 408
Canada 13, 20
Canadian 13
carpe diem 390
Chant of the Fianna 424
children 44, 45, 46, 47
Christ 208, 239, 241
Christian 214
clash 301

clear 269
clever 428
comes 397, 421
comfort 258
confidence 336
confident 337
conqueror 270
Corinthians 159, 160, 161, 162
country 410
courage 271, 338
courageous 339
cousin 48, 49
crone 209

D

Dad 50
Daddy 51, 52
dance 306, 369
dancer 307
darling 52, 169,
daughter 52, 53, 54, 55, 56, 58,
        61, 103, 104, 130
daughters 54, 57, 59, 60, 62,
        63, 64
day 379, 390, 421
dead 420
dear 34, 74, 89, 101, 113,
death 258, 272, 273, 296
deeds 424
demons 201
departed 187, 192, 194
devil 210, 420
devils 211
die 371
dishonour 273
doctor 308
dream 371
drug-free 372
druid 212, 213

E

earth 198, 247
easy 394
endearment 169
enduring 415
enemies 258
Ephesians 233
eternal 164, 166, 167, 168, 177,
        178, 179
eternally 135, 290
evening 421
ever 138
everlasting 136, 215
everything 373
evil 216, 228, 247, 258,
Exodus 93
eyes 384, 385, 398, 399

F

faith 70, 161, 217, 233
faithful 290
family 65, 66, 67, 68, 69, 70,
fate 222
father 71, 72, 73, 74, 76, 77, 93,
        94, 107, 130, 218, 219,
        220, 221, 247
fatherhood 75
fear 258, 387
few 405
Fianna 424
fiddler 309
fire 198
firefighter 310
fireside 426
first 67
fisherman 311
fled 301
flies 375, 391
follow 258, 274

force 404
forever 7, 35, 68, 69, 114, 137,
        138, 141, 197, 247, 258,
        290, 371
forgive 247
forgiveness 70
free 340, 372
freedom 341
friend 39, 40, 41, 42, 118, 119,
        120, 121, 139, 142, 144,
        145, 164, 165, 411
friends 140, 141, 142, 166
friendship 146, 147, 148
fullest 381

G

gambler 312
girl 14, 52, 57, 402,
girls 57
glory 247
God 173, 182, 183, 184, 185,
        186, 204, 223, 231, 232,
        389, 416, 418
goddess 226
goddesses 227
gods 224, 225
goes 397
good 228, 354, 412, 413
goodness 229, 258
grace 230, 231, 232, 233
grandchild 78
grandchildren 79
granddad 85
granddaughter 80
granddaughters 81
grandfather 82, 83, 84
grandma 90
grandmother 86, 87, 88, 89
grandpa 85

grandson 91
grandsons 92
granny 90
great 419
greatest 161, 162
ground 374

H

hallowed 251
hallowed 247
hand 182, 183, 184, 185, 186,
        208, 418
handsome 126, 127, 128, 129
happiness 342
happy 343
hardship 411
harm 202
harper 313
harpist 313
harvest 419
hatred 344
healer 383
healing 345
health 417
heart 5, 6, 16, 23, 157, 169, 175,
        176, 197, 208, 275
hearts 176, 424
heaven 234, 247, 420
hell 235
help 416
heritage 1
hero 275, 277, 278
heroes 279, 280
heroine 281, 282
heroines 283, 284
hold 182, 374, 418
holy 219, 220, 22, 236, 237, 238
Holy Spirit 219, 220, 221, 237
home 426

homesickness 2
honour 93, 94, 95, 285
hope 346
hopeful 347
hunter 315
hurt 378
husband 149, 150, 151, 152

I

infantry 274
Infinite 349
infinity 348
innocent 406
Ireland 4, 5, 6, 7, 21, 23
Irish 3, 8, 9, 10, 11, 12, 13, 14,
        18, 19, 20, 22, 24, 384,
        385, 398, 399, 418
Irish-American 11
Irish-Canadian 13
Irish Blessing 195, 418
island 422

J

Jesus 240, 241, 242, 243
Joseph 242, 243, 244
joy 350
joyful 351
judge 389
justice 410

K

keeper 43
kill 395
kind 159
kingdom 247

L

lad 12
land 15, 16, 17,
language 410
lass 14
laugh 380
laughter 356, 424
life 47, 60, 215, 258, 352, 380,
        381, 400
little 423
live 371, 379, 380, 381, 382,
        400, 403, 422
lives 414
long 403, 414, 421
longing 2
lord 245, 246, 247, 254, 258,
        407, 409
Lord of the Rings 407
Lord's Prayer 247
lost 407
love 6, 134, 147, 148, 153, 154,
        155, 157, 158, 159, 160,
        161, 162, 167, 168, 169,
        378, 380,
lovely 402
lover 156
loving 189
loyalty 148,
luck 353, 354
lucky 3, 355

M

made 19, 20, 21, 22, 402
magic 248
maiden 249
Mammy (Mommy) 97
man 422, 429
many 405, 425
Marine 290

Mark (book of the Bible) 173
Mary (mother of Jesus) 242,
        243, 250, 252
meet 195, 255, 418
memory 189
men 419
mercy 253, 254, 258
mermaid 316
merry 255
middle 37, 116
mighty 357
miss 181, 196
Mom 96
Momma 97
Mommy 97
mote 259
mother 93, 95, 98, 99, 100, 101,
        103, 104, 105, 106, 107,
        130,
music 317, 381, 383
musician 318
myself 377

N

name 221, 247, 258, 413
needs 405,
never 160, 301, 378, 406
nevertheless 386
New York's Fighting 69th
Regiment 269, 301
nostalgia 2
nurse 319, 320

O

oil 258
oldest 36, 115
Oregon 375, 391
Our Father 247
outweigh 405

P

pagan 256
Papa (Daddy) 51
paradise 257
parents 108
part 255
partner (romantic) 163
pass 396
patient 159
Patrick (Saint) 208
patriot 287
patriotism 288
peace 286, 358, 359
people 65, 422
persisted 386
Philippians (book of the Bible)
        239
piper 321
pirate 322
place 426
poet 323
power 247, 360
powerful 361
praises 429
prayer 247, 408
pride 362
professor 324
prosper 403
prosperity 363
protect 289
proud 24, 364
Psalms (book of the Bible) 204,
        258
pulse 169

R

rain 418
reader 305
reap 381, 419
reason 373
Rede 202
regret 388
regrets 388
rest 177, 178, 179, 180
riches 413
ride 382
righteousness 258
road 418
run 412

S

sacred 236
sacrifice 365
sailor 325
saint 244, 208
salvation 261
saved 233, 262
saviour 263, 264, 265
say 423
secret 169
seize 390
selkie 316
Semper Fidelis 290
sense 430
serve 289
shadow 258, 422
shepherd 258
shepherds 409
shine 418
shining 169
sin 247
sing 393
singer 326
sinner 260

sins 247
sister 109, 111, 112, 113, 115, 116, 117, 118, 119, 120, 121
sisters 110, 114
smiling 384, 385, 398, 399
soldier 291, 292
soldiers 293, 294
son 76, 77, 105, 106, 122, 123, 124, 126, 130, 219, 220, 221
Song of Solomon/Song of Songs (book of the Bible) 131, 132, 133
sons 125, 127, 128, 129
sorrow 2, 402
soul 17, 183, 184, 186, 258, 383, 410
soulmate 164, 165, 167, 168
soulmates 166
souls 185
spirit 219, 220, 221, 237
spouse 163, 167, 168
stand 374, 412
Star Trek 403, 405
Star Wars 404
still 204, 258
strength 367, 424
strong 367, 428
stronger 395
success 368
sun 418
swords 301

T

take 390, 394
teacher 327
temptation 247
terms of endearment 169

today 371
Tolkien, J.R.R. 407
tradition 25
treasure 169
trinity 238
truth 401, 187, 192, 194
twist 425

U

U.S.A. 11, 22
U.S. Army Infantry 274
U.S. Marine Corps 290
United States 22
unity 427

V

vegetarian 328
veritas 401, 430
victor 270
victory 295, 296
vino 430
virgin 251, 252

W

walk 258
walks 376
wander 407
want 258
warrior 276, 297, 298
warriors 299, 300
water 198, 258
way 187, 192, 194, 269,
wealth 415, 417
Wiccan 202
wicked 406
wife 152, 170, 171, 172, 173
wild 408
will 202, 247

wind 418
wine 430
wings 375, 391
word 415, 424
work 429
world 47, 60

Y

YOLO 400
youngest 38, 117

Other titles in the
TATTOO HANDBOOK
SERIES

More from **bradan press**

| Nonfiction books about Scottish Gaelic language and culture | Scottish Gaelic translations of *Anne of Green Gables* and other classics | Fionn MacCool and other Gaelic and Celtic children's books |

www.bradanpress.com

Printed in Great Britain
by Amazon

51577864R00061